The author has worked laboriously and unceasingly, in order to produce this first class Dream Book. He has traveled all over the world so as to gather correct data. There is nothing miraculously attached to this book: It is truly a dream book of the highest order. You will find the interpretation of dreams to be the very best. The Horoscope is so condensed, that it enables you to get all the main facts of your life at a glance.

There are so many people who desire to get a concise definition of a dream. A dream is the forecast of coming events. It generally comes to us in a parable, or in some other similar form during sleep. It is therefore, quite necessary to consult a good dream book. A dream is really a warning of coming events, whether favorable or unfavorable.

By Professor De HERBERT

Printed in the U. S. A.

HOLIDAYS

Armistice Day **085**

Christmas **250**

Columbus Day **661**

Decoration Day **674**

Easter **219**

Election Day **365**

Good Friday **733**

Whitsuntide **309**

Labor Day **735**

Lincoln's Birthday **564**

New Year's Day **890**

St. Patrick's Day **830**

Thanksgiving **725**

Washington's Birthday **596**

Independence Day **469**

369
485

ABBESS—To dream of an abbess denotes that you will make a great sacrifice in the behalfs of humanity. **311**

ABBEY—Denotes sadness, generally some relative is about to die. **411**

To visit an abbey is a sign of popularity among the elite. **871**

ABDOMEN—To dream of the abdomen is a sign of flattery. **334**

ABUNDANCE—To dream of having plenty of anything, denotes scarcity in that particular commodity. **315**

ABNORMAL—To dream an abnormal person is a sign of weakness and inability to conduct business advantageously. **781**

To quarrel with an abnormal person is a sign of happiness. **911**

ABORTION—To dream of an abortion denotes danger from an unexpected source. **924**

ABROAD—To travel abroad denotes courage and much happiness. **181**

To dream of seeing others going abroad is a sign of sudden wealth and enjoyment among friends. **791**

ABSENT—To dream of going abroad denotes that you will suffer loss on account of your own negligence. **448**

ABSENT-MINDED—To dream that you see an absent-minded person denotes that your memory is becoming keener than ever. This means that you can remember anything without any great amount of effort. Your learning ability is improving rapidly. **356**

ABUSIVE—To dream of an abusive person denotes that you will be the victim of discrimination. **937**

To abuse any one is a sign of distrust on your part. **367**

ACADEMIC COURSE—To dream of taking this

course promises a great deal of prosperity and
good health. It also denotes intelligence. **569**

ACCIDENT—To see one in your sleep, denotes losses
to the rich, and prosperity to the poor. **382**

ACCOUNTANCY—To dream of this course in a sign
that riches and honor will be thrown upon you in
the near future. **381**

ACTIVITY—This dream indicates that the dreamer
understands human weaknesses to perfection. It
is a sign that the dreamer possesses unlimited
experience, and by so doing he is in a position to
help his fellow-men. **215**

ACCURACY—To dream of performing a duty with
perfection is a sign of sudden wealth, generally
luck in all kinds of games of chances. **536**

ACCUSATION—To dream that you are being accused
for any kind of an act, denotes danger of little consequence. **500**

To dream of accusing any one is a sign of power
and dignity. **111**

ACHIEVEMENT—To dream of an achievement denotes that you will succeed in all of your undertaking no matter what they happen to be. This
dream warns you to proceed with that which you
desire to accomplish. **628**

To dream of seeing others succeed in their undertaking, denotes that you will become very popular
in your community and be happy for the rest of
your life. **590**

ACID—To dream of any kind of acid denotes that you
will suceed in carrying out your plans. **311**

ACQUAINTANCE—To dream that you are being in-
troduced to a strange person, is a sign that you
receive the letter that you had anticipated. **469**

ACROBAT—To see one in your sleep is a sign that
you are going to visit one whom you have not
seen for many years. **711**

To talk to one shows that you will have strange experience shortly, yet no harm will come to you. 621

ACTOR—To see one denotes that you will be called upon to be the leader in your community. You are a born leader. 534

ACTRESS—To see one upon the stage denotes that your sweet heart loves you dearly. 672
To enjoy the play of an actress is a sign of wealth followed by much happiness. 725

ACUTE INDIGESTION—This dream is a warning of your eating. You should have a well selected diet in order to off-set the attack of indigestion. 918

ADDRESS—To dream of writing the address of any one is a sign of courtship which will end in a happy marriage followed by many handsome children, generally three boys and two girls. 641

ADMIRAL—To see one in your sleep indicates high social standard. 349
To talk to one is a sign of power and dignity. 911

ADMIRE—To admire anyone is a sign of affection, generally from a beautiful young person. 385

ADORE—To adore any one denotes that you will be married shortly. This marriage will lift you far above your present position in life. 611
To be adored denotes sudden wealth. 351

ADRIFT—To see any one adrift denotes loneliness of short duration. 411

ADULTERY—To dream that you commit adultery is a sign of sorrow followed by an abundance of pleasure. 135

ADVERTISE—To advertise is a sign of prudence. It indicates that you are a good business person. 349

ADVICE—To give advice denotes that you will be wrongly accused for something in which you have not taken any part in. You should be very careful in the manner in which you conduct yourself. **645**

AEROPLANE—Denotes that you will rise to a high position in life and that you will be happy and prosperous throughout the succeeding years of your life. **161**

To see one crash denotes that one of your friends is a little indisposed. This friend is greatly in need of your assistance. **751**

To see one go into a dive denotes joy. **215**

AFFIDAVIT—To make an affidavit, denotes courage and will power. **113**

AFRAID—To dream of being afraid is a sign of danger from an unexpected source. **501**

To dream that anyone is afraid of you is a sign of supremacy. **116**

AGENT—To dream that you are an agent for any commodity, denotes that you should accept the position that is offered to you. **812**

AGGRAVATE—To be aggravated is a sign that some one will persuade you to invest money in an unreliable concern. **364**

AGITATOR—To see one in your sleep denotes shame and remorse. **161**

To quarrel with one, denotes that you will succeed in conducting your business advantageously. **718**

AGONY—To dream of being in agony of pain denotes regrets. To see others suffering is a sign of remorse. **465**

AGUE—Is a sign that your friends are unfaithful. It also denotes trouble and vexation of spirit. **065**

AGRICULTURE—To dream of farming, promises good luck on the following day. You are going to have a fair sum of money shortly. This money will be derived from games of chances. **204**

AIR PUMP—Denotes that you will travel shortly. Your voyage will be one of much happiness. **911**

ALARM—To be alarmed in your sleep is a sign that

you will be the recipient of exciting news, which will work out to your utmost satisfaction. **745**

ALCOHOL—To dream of drinking alcohol is a sign of much pleasure. **111**
To manufacture it, is a sign of sudden wealth. **371**
To buy it denotes popularity. **311**

ALE HOUSE—To see one in your sleep denotes an unfortunate marriage. **919**

ALGEBRA—To dream of working out problems in algebra is a sign of wealth and much happiness throughout the succeeding years of your life. **769**

ALIEN—To dream of an alien denotes that you will visit a sick person shortly. **724**

ALLEY—To dream of being in an alley, signifies that that you are going to visit a scene of intense solemnity. **419**

ALL FOOLS DAY—To dream of this day is a sign of domestic troubles which will not last. **734**

ALLIGATOR—To dream of this man-eating fish is a sign of accident of little consequence. **717**

ALMANAC—To see one in your sleep denotes that you will make a very important date with one whom you had the least expectation to meet. **639**

ALMHOUSE—To dream of one denotes poverty and sickness. **135**

ALMS—To give alms denotes everlasting prosperity. This is a very good dream to those who are planning to go into a new enterprise. **402**

ALMONDS—To dream of ripe almonds, signify prosperity; young almonds denote misfortune. **716**

ALOES—To dream of taking aloes signifies that you are going to receive a letter which will contain sad news. **918**

ALONE—To dream of being alone denotes that you will rise to a higher position in life. **138**

ALPHABET—To dream of the alphabet indicates great learning which will place you far above your present position. **761**

ALTAR—To dream of going to the altar is a sure sign of engagement followed by a quick but prosperous marriage. **811**

To see others at the altar denotes ambition. **911**

ALUM—To dream of taking alum is a sign of discrimination. Do not go where you are not wanted. **717**

AMAZE—To dream that you are amazed at anything is a sign that you will receive a letter shortly which will contain good news. To dream of seeing others amazed denotes that you will be slandered. **792**

AMBASSADOR—To see one in your sleep denotes long life and prosperity. **831**

To talk to an ambassador denotes benevolence. **319**

AMBULANCE—To see one in your sleep denotes sickness. To drive in one is a sign that you will visit one of your friends who is now indisposed. To see others in one, denotes mischief. **555**

AMMONIA—To dream of ammonia denotes that you are going to be the recipient of a good paying position. It also indicates that you are going to raise a large sum of money from this position.**744**

AMMUNITION—To dream of ammunition, denotes that you will have a misunderstanding with some one. You should be very careful not to engage in a fight. **802**

AMMUNITION PLANT—To visit one denotes riches in abundance. To work in one is a sign of large profits. **367**

AMUSEMENTS—To dream of any kind of amusements is a sign of long life and prosperity, accompanied by loving and sincere friends. **538**

ANALYSIS—To analize anything denotes that you will discover a startling truth about a certain affair in which you were much interested. **231**

ANCESTORS—To dream of any of your ancestors is a sign that you will receive a letter from afar which will contain good news. If you do not talk to them in your sleep, it indicates grief and anxiety of short duration. **761**

ANCHOR—Denotes slow progress, but that you will succeed eventually and live happily. **644**

ANGEL—To dream of one denotes happiness and long life. **752**

ANGER—To dream that you get into a rage, denotes that you are in company with notorious characters. You should therefore change your company. **960**

ANKLE—To dream of one denotes that you will travel a fair distance on foot. **398**

ANNIVERSARY—To dream of any kind of an anniversary, denotes that you will perform an act of heroism for which you will be greatly rewarded. Your name will therefore live on through the ages. **637**

ANNOY—To dream of being annoyed denotes disaster. **223**

To annoy any one is a sign of popularity among the aristocrats. **231**

ANTHEM—To chant one in your sleep denotes a loving wife, husband, or sweetheart. It denotes that you are at peace with the world. **214**

ANTS—To dream of ants denotes a great deal of money. If they bite you, it is a sign of marked prosperity. **302**

ANTIQUE—To dream of anything that is old, denotes that your secret which you have guarded so long, will be revealed. Nevertheless you will not suffer any uneasiness from it. **303**

APARTMENT—To dream of having a well furnished apartment denotes sadness. A poorly furnished apartment is a sign of wealth and everlasting health. **080**

APE—To dream of one, denotes that you will be the victim of slander. **631**

APOLOGY—To apologize to any one in your sleep, denotes a week mind, but a loving disposition. **837**

APPENDICITIS—Is a sign of vexation of short duration. **318**

APPETITE—To dream that your appetite is decreasing, denotes that it is increasing, and vice-versa. **365**

APPLE—To see one in your sleep denotes riches if ripe; poverty if young. **549**

To sell apples denote a contented life. **943**

To give them away is a sign of health followed by years of prosperity. **534**

APPRAISER—To dream of one denotes poverty for a few years. **817**

APRON—Denotes that you will enjoy the picture of good health. To the sick it promises the return to good health accompanied by a great deal of prosperity. **473**

ARAB—To dream of one denotes domestic troubles. **511**

ARCH—To see one in your sleep denotes great success. It also denotes that through your genius and learning you will recover your losses. **367**

ARCH-BISHOP—To dream of an arch-bishop is a sign of popularity which will make you the leader in society, and many other business enterprises. **636**

ARCHITECT—To see one in your sleep denotes that you will succeed in paying the mortgage on your home, after a little struggle. **891**

ARGUMENT—To dream of argumentation denotes that you are misjudging your friend's character. **143**

ARITHMETIC—To dream of arithmetic signifies that

you are familiar with human weakness. **249**

It also denotes that you will come in contact with a prominent person. **243**

ARM CHAIR—To dream of an arm chair signifies that you will soon be able to put your feet against the stove, and smoke a big cigar through the cold wintry months, while the world toils on. You are going to be comfortably rich. **821**

ARMISTICE DAY—To dream of this blessed day is a sign of peace and prosperity accompanied by the picture of good health. **500**

ARMORY—To dream of one, denotes that some one is very jealous of your progress. **555**

ARMS—To dream of powerful arms indicate an honorable career; much success is in store for you. **659**

ARMY—To see an army denotes shelter to the homeless. **312**

To see an army in action denotes danger. **281**

ARREST—To dream of an arrest is a sign of vexation. **303**

ARROW ROOT—To dream of the plant or of the starch, denotes that you are going to move into better quarters shortly. **136**

ARSENIC—Is a sign that the prisoner will be speedily released. **194**

ARTIFICIAL—To dream of anything that is artificial is a sign that you are being deceived **571.**

ARTILLERY—To the dreamer it denotes temptation. **937**

ARTIST—To see one in your sleep denotes an abundance of pleasure. It also indicates great success in all of your present undertakings. **115**

ASCEND—To go up any place denotes success in all your undertaking. To dream that you are unable to reach your destination denotes failure. **603**

ASHES—To dream of ashes denotes reverses in business. Take care how you transact your affairs, both at home and abroad. **912**

ASPARAGUS—Denotes an honorable and marked career. It also indicates that you will enjoy good health. This is indeed a very pleasant dream. **363**

ASSASSINATION—To witness one signifies embarrassment. It also denotes cowardice. **167**

ASSEMBLYMAN—To dream of one denotes that you will get the position you desire, some day. **294**

ASTROLOGER—To talk with one mark his words and do according to his instruction. This is a dream of observation. **487**

ASYLUM—To dream of one denotes sickness. **732**

ATHEIST—To see one in your sleep denotes that your character will be questioned by your church members. **264**

AUTHOR—To see one at work denotes that you will receive a declaration of love from your sweetheart. It also indicates profitable investments. **725**

ATTACK—To dream of being attacked denotes destruction of your plans, lost hope. **711**

ATTORNEY GENERAL—To talk to him is a sign of law suit in which you will win after a terrific struggle. **617**

AUCTION BRIDGE—Denotes that you are going to take your place in society, it also indicates that you are going to be the life of all parties that you attend. **765**

AUCTIONEER—Denotes poverty and sickness. **749**

AUDITOR—To see ont in your sleep is a sign of sudden wealth. **365**

AUTOMOBILE—To dream of one denotes that you are going to rise far above your present position in life and be happy. **733**

AVIATOR—To see one in your sleep denotes that you will own a great deal of property in the near future. **278**

BABY—To dream of a baby denotes an abundance
of health and wealth. **211**
To see many babies denote that you are dearly loved
by your wife or husband. **112**

BABY CARRIAGE—Denotes sudden joy and much
prosperity. **897**

BABY FARM—To see one in your sleep denotes that
you will succeed in getting the position that you
desire. This position will bring you a fairly decent
sum of money which you will invest wisely and
make more money. **219**

BABOON—To see one in your sleep signifies that you
will commit a silly act in order to amuse others.
725

BACK—To dream that your back has grown larger
than normal signifies sudden wealth. **734**

BACK-BITE—To dream that some one is slandering
you is a sign of domestic troubles. **933**

BACK SLIDE—To back slide denotes that a charge
will be brought against you to the denomination
in which you are now a member. Do not worry,
this charge will be dismissed immediately. **402**

BACON—To dream of eating bacon signifies that you
will be happily married in the near future. **181**
To buy it signifies prominence. **176**
To give it away is a sign of love affairs. **781**

BACKYARD—To dream of being in your backyard,
is a sign of wealth acocmpanied by extremely good
health. If you walk in a strange backyard, it denotes a trip, either by land or sea. **104**

BADGE—To see one in your sleep, denotes that you
will hold an important position in government
service. **861**
To see others wearing a badge, denotes haste. **679**

BAG—An empty bag, denotes dishonor. **391**
A filled bag is a sign of health and the picture
of universal prosperity. **417**

BAGPIPES—To see them in your sleep, denotes joy and profit. **642**

BAIL—To dream that you stand bail for any one, denotes security in all of your business transactions. **297**

If another stands bail for you, it is a sign of uncomfortable circumstances. **761**

BAKER—To see one at work signifies small gains. **717**

To quarrel with a baker is a sign of economic depression of short duration. **712**

BAKERY—To visit one signifies that your parents have a large sum of money for you, along with other property. **164**

BAKING—To dream of baking is a sign of popularity among friends and other acquaintances. **728**

BAKING POWDER—To dream of baking-powder is a sign of universal festivity and social enjoyment. **914**

BALCONY—To dream of a balcony is a sign of love affairs, followed by everlasting and peaceful happiness. **734**

BALD HEAD—To dream of a bald head is a sign of unhappiness, followed by a little pleasure. **217**

BALL-ROOM—To see one in your sleep signifies a happy, peaceful existence. It indicates a happy ending of all your troubles, and a reunion among friends and relatives. **791**

BALOON—To dream of a baloon denotes that you will rise to an esteem position in life and live happily ever after. To see one but not enter, signifies a speedy journey of relative importance. **535**

BALSAM—To dream of balsam denotes the birth of a baby boy, **763**

BAMBOO—To see a great deal of Bamboo, signifies that you are fond of hunting games of all kinds. **586**

BANDAGE—To dream of a bandage, is a sign of mischief, which will be attributed to your loose conduct. **583**

BANDIT—To see one in your sleep is a sign of approaching danger from an unexpected source. **607** To catch the bandit signifies that you will foul your enemies at their own game. **738**

BANK—To dream of a bank is a sign that your savings will grow by and by. **324**

BANKER—To dream of a banker signifies that you will accumulate a great deal of money as the years roll on. **391**

BANISHMENT—To dream of being banished is a sign that some one in whom you are much interested, is a little indisposed. **356**

BANQUET—To dream of a banquet denotes joy and profit. **378**

BAPTISM—To witness one denotes that you are a religious person, faithful and true in all your dealings. **323**

BAREFOOT—To dream of being barefoot is a sign of aggravation, which cannot be avoided by you. **291**

BAREHEADED—To dream of walking bareheaded is a sign that you are leading a sporty life. **364**

BARELEGGED—To see shapely bare legs is a sign of temptation. **783**

BARGE—To see one in your sleep denotes a trip across water. To see one drifting at random is a sign of vexation. **128**

BAR KEEPER—To see one in your sleep is a sign of drunkeness. **362**

BARLEY—To see barley denotes riches in abundance. **942** To eat it is a sign of long life and prosperity and domestic happiness. **207**

BARN—An empty barn signifies wealth. **469**

A filled barn denotes approaching marriage. **697**

BAROMETER—To dream of one is a sign that you are about to change your present abode for quarters, much befitting your social position, and prestige. **418**

BARREL—To dream of a filled barrel denotes, wealth. **369**

An empty one denotes losses. **121**

BASE-BALL—To dream of playing base-ball is a sign that you will live to a good old age, and then die happily. **945**

To see others play this game is a sign of peace and satisfaction. **567**

BASIN—To see one is a sign of sickness. **203**

To see a basin filled with clear water denotes cleanliness. **305**

An unclean basin, denotes sorrow. **300**

BASKET—A filled basket signifies, that you will receive a declaration of love from your sweetheart. **767**

BASKET BALL GAME—To dream of seeing or partaking in this sport denotes long life and much prosperity. **462**

BAT—To see one in your sleep is a sign that your eye-sight is getting bad. This dream warns you to wear glasses at once. Delay may result in the loss of your eyesight. **434**

BATH—To dream that you take a bath is a sign of pleasure. **897**

To see others bathing is a sign of skill and successful business enterprises. **227**

BATHTUB—To see one in your sleep, signifies that you will succeed in executing your present plans. **911**

BATH ROBE—To dress in a beautiful bath robe is a sign of domestic happines. To see another person dressed in a bath robe indicates jealousy. **985**

BAYONET—Denotes that you will engage in a controversy with one in power. **972**

BAY RUM—To see it in your sleep deotes that you will succeed in executing your plans. **712**
To rub with it is a sign of devotion. **234**

BEACH—To dream that you visit the beach promises peace and satisfaction. **862**

BEACON—To dream of beacon is a sign of courage. **567**

BEADS—To dream of beads denote that you will be called upon to act in an important situation, which will not only bring you popularity, but also wealth. **716**

BEANS—To dream of beans is a sign of worries and vexation. **723**

BEARD—To dream of having a long beard denotes long life and prosperity. **613**
White beard denotes a successful career. **139**
Grey beard signifies a successsful marriage. **691**
If a woman dreams of having a beard, it indicates love affairs, and much happiness. **090**

BEAR—To see one denotes graft and plunder. **433**

RED BUG—To see one in your sleep, denotes secret enemies. **762**

BED-ROOM—To dream of a well furnished bedroom denotes that you are the master or the mistress of your own affairs. Do not let any one conduct your business, because you have the ability to act at the right time. **697**

BEEF—To see a great deal of beef, denotes that you will have a funeral, generally a relative or dear friend. **225**

BEER—To dream of beer denotes that you will rise to an important position in your community shortly. **767**

BEES—To see them in your sleep signify prosperity, regardless of your present position. **361**

To dream of honey bees denote long life and prosperity. **634**

BEGGAR—To dream of a beggar signifies that you are the master or mistress of extra-ordinary sagacity. **632**

To give alms to a beggar signifies that you will be elevated to a prominent position in life, which will be attributed to your genius and learning. **219**

BEHEAD—To see a person beheaded denotes that you will be falsely accused, and it will cost you a great deal of money and effort to escape being punished. **718**

BELL—To hear one ring signifies that you are studious and sincere. **524**

BERRIES—To dream of ripe berries, denote good fortune. Green berries, bad luck on the following day. **975**

BIRDS—Denote success in your present undertakings. **181**

BIRDS NEST—To see young birds in a nest is a sign of much happiness. It indicates good luck in games of chances. **211**

BISCUITS—To dream of brown biscuits signify gain. White biscuits is a sign of loss. **527**

BLOOD—Denotes sorrow and vexation. **518**

BLOOMER—To see one is a sign of joy and profit. **837**

BLOSSOM—Denotes new hopes followed by peace and good health. **934**

BOARDING SCHOOL—To see one in your sleep, denotes sudden joy and much profit. **224**

BOARD-WALK—To dream of a board-walk, signifies that you will go on a vacation shortly. **872**

BOBBED HAIR—To dream that your hair is bobbed signifies a great deal of pleasure. **305**

To see others with bobbed hair denotes that you will succeed in executing your plans. **315**

BODYGUARD—To see one is a sign of protection. **915**

BOILER—To dream of one is a sign that you will move to better quarters shortly. **823**

BOLSHEVISM—To dream of this doctrine is a sign of economic slavery. **738**

BOLT—To see one denotes that you will be caught stealing something of non-importance. **634**

BOMB—To see one explode denotes danger and reverse in business. **523**

BONDSMAN—To talk to one is a sign of trouble in which you will escape after paying a great deal of graft. **900**

BOOKKEEPER—To dream of a bookkeeper denotes that you will conduct a huge and prosperous business in the near future. **257**

BOOKMAKER—Denotes sudden wealth. It also indicates that the sick will recover shortly. **721**

BOOTLEGGER—To dream that you are a bootlegger denotes that you will make big dough shortly. **970** To see others in this money making racket, denotes prosperity. **798**

BOSS—To dream of being a boss, signifies that you will occupy an important position of no mean capacity in your community. **734**

BOW-LEGGED—To dream of a bow-legged person denotes that you will be greatly embarrassed. To dream that you are bow-legged signifies a pleasant surprise. **515**

BOTTLE—To dream of a filled bottle denotes pleasure and the picture of good health, providing that you do not drink too much. **297**

BRACELET—To see one in your sleep denotes that you will meet your lover shortly, and that you will be happily married. **131**

To lose your bracelet denotes secret sorrows. **729**

BREAD—To dream of bread signifies an abundance

of wealth and happiness. **923**

BREAKFAST—To dream of taking breakfast signifies
that you will succeed in all of your undertakings,
regardless of conditions. **497**

BRIBERY—To dream that you are being bribed denotes financial assistance. **501**

To dream that you try to bribe another person is a
sign of power and dignity. **367**

BRICKS—To dream of bricks denote that you will
be the very best dresser in your community in
the near future. **725**

BRIDE—To see one in your sleep signifies a happy
ending of all your troubles. **385**

BRIDGE—A stone bridge signifies a profitable investment. **314**

A wooden bridge denotes distress. **718**

BROOCH—Denotes that your sweetheart is true to
you. This is truly an excellent and inspiring dream
to lovers. **781**

BROTHER—Is a sign of joy and prosperity. **134**

To quarrel with your brother denotes sad news. **561**

BROTHER-IN-LAW—To dream of your brother-in-
law denotes that you will not succeed in executing
your plans. **293**

BRUSH—To see one in your sleep denotes that you
are of a cowardly nature, yet you are loving and
kind. **381**

BUCKET—To see a filled bucket denotes sudden
wealth. **378**

An empty bucket denotes dishonor. **769**

BUILDING—One built of stones denotes riches in
abundance. One built of wood is a sign of adversity. **748**

BULL—To dream of a bull denotes that you will be
engaged in a fight. **874**

BULLET—To dream of a bullet denotes an unsatis-
fied mind. **124**

BUMBLEBEE—To see one in your sleep denotes that you will soon reap the sweets of your labor. **736**

BUNIONS—To dream of bunions denote riches in proportion to the bunions. To see others affected by bunions denote that your friends are sincere. **705**

BUS BOY—To dream of a bus boy denotes that you will be in a position to hire help shortly. **278**

BUTCHER—To see one in your sleep denotes wealth and power followed by extraordinary good health. **301**

BUTTER—To see a great deal of butter signifies that your wife or husband loves you dearly. **119**

BUTTONS—To see a great deal of buttons indicate that prosperity is just around the corner. **936**

BUYING—To dream of buying anything, denotes marked prosperity. **201**

CAB—To dream of riding in a cab signifies that you are going to perform duty of the highest order. You will be greatly honored for your service. **271** To see others driving in a cab signifies much happiness. **564**

CABARET—To visit one signifies that you are wasting your time visiting that young man or young woman. **394**

CABBAGE—Denotes secret enemies. **211**
To dream that you cook or eat it is a sign of lost hope. **269**

CABIN—To see one denotes low circumstances. **783** To see a great deal of people in a cabin is a sign of freedom. Your wife or husband is going to grant you your desire. **351**

CABLEGRAM—To dream of one signifies that some dear to you is trying to locate you. **591**

CAGE—To see a bird in a cage signifies that one of your friends' liberty is threatened. **173**

CAIBRE—To see one in your sleep denotes distress. **412**

CAKE—To eat it denotes sudden wealth. To turn away from it denotes poverty. **410**

CALENDAR—To dream of a calendar, signifies that you will make an important date with your lover. **283**

CALF—To see a young calf at its mother's breast, signifies that you will receive a declaration of love from your sweetheart. **593**

CALICO—To wear it denotes poverty of short duration. **311**
To see others dressed in calico denotes that a member of your family is a little indisposed. **851**

CAMEL—To see one denotes a pleasant journey from which you will gain a great deal of experience. This trip is an education for you. **512**

CAMPHOR—Denotes a dangerous disease is about to attack you. You should therefore guard yourself against coming in contact with people who are sick. **731**

CAMP FIRE—To see one burning is a sign of fortune and the picture of good health. **205**
To dream that you are unable to keep a camp fire burning bright indicates failure in your present undertakings. **673**

CANCER—To dream of seeing any one with the sick, denotes lost hopes. **183**

CANDLE—To see one burning bright indicates a brilliant future. If it is burning dim, it denotes sad news. **513**

CANDY—To see a great deal of candy denotes pregnancy. **171**
To a man it signifies that his wife is pregnant, and that she will have a baby boy who will be a successful business man. **935**

CANNON—To see or hear one roar denotes misunderstanding among friends and other associates. **515**

CANOE—Denotes change of address. **318**

CANTALOUPES—Is a sign of wealth and much happiness throughout the coming years. **085**

CAP—To dream of one denotes loss of goods. To wear one deceit and treachery. **314**

CAPTAIN—To dream of a man who is a captain of any affair is a sign of power and executive ability. It denotes a rise in position right away. **471**

CAPTURE—To dream of being captured is a sign of suffering. To capture any one denotes power and prestige. **813**

CAR—To ride in one denotes joy and profit. To see others ride in one indicates success in business. **312**

CARDS—To dream of playing cards signify that your ambition will be realized. You are going to succeed in executing your plans in every way. **182**

CARGO—Sgnifies an abundance of wealth and much happiness. **042**

CARNIVAL—To see one in your sleep portrays sudden wealth. **018**

CARPENTER—To dream of one denotes fairly good circumstances. **752**

CARRIAGE—To ride in one denotes happiness. A broken carriage denotes misfortune. **481**

CARROTS—To dream of carrots denote that a stranger is going to ask a favor of you. This stranger will become one of your best friends. **375**

CARTRIDGE—To dream of a cartridge denotes danger from an unexpected source. **511**

CASH REGISTER—To see one in your sleep denotes that you are going to conduct a well paying business in the near future. **371**

CASHIER—To see a pretty cashier denotes a successful marriage. A homely cashier denotes loss of reputation. **643**

CASK OF WINE—To see a cask of wine in your sleep foretells that you will receive a declaration of love from your sweetheart. **481**

CASKET—Denotes loss by fire. To see them being made is a sign of dishonor and discontent. **519**

CASTOR OIL—To dream of castor oil is a sign of ill health. **711**
To see others take it denotes that you wll be the victim of slander and notoriety. **325**

CAT—To see a black cat is a sign of approaching danger. **144**
To dream of a brown or ashes color cat is a sign of happiness. **615**

CATHEDRAL—To visit one denotes that you will visit a scene of historical eminence. **418**

CATHOLIC—To dream of a Catholic denotes trouble from one whom you have always trusted. **671**
To quarrel with one signifies that your enemies are more than a match for you. **834**

CATTLE—To see a great deal of cattle in your sleep is a sign of long life and prosperity. **523**

CAVALRY—To dream of a cavalry signifies that you will be called upon to fill an important position. **235**

CAVE—To dream that you visit one denotes that you will be called away from home on a business transaction. **367**

CELERY—To dream of celery denotes that you are a little too hasty in judging others. **789**

CELL—To dream of a cell is a sign that you will experience a little inconvenience. **345**

CELLAR—To dream of a cellar denotes that you will save a great deal of money shortly. **193**

CEMENT—To dream of a great quantity of cement, denotes hardship and vexation of spirit. **971**

CEMETERY—Denotes shrewd business enterprise. **392**

CEREMONY—To dream of a ceremony denotes a funeral. It also indicates power of patience and the steadfastness of purpose. 301

CERTIFICATE—To dream that you possess any kind of certificate is a sign that you will fall heir to a small legacy at the death of a relative or sincere friend. 737

CHAIN—A gold chain denotes success in business. 418

A silver chain is a sign of disappointment. 445

Any other kind of a chain is a sign of security in all business transactions. 456

CHAIN STORE—To visit one signifies that you will get the job that you desire. 173

CHANGING MONEY—Foretells that you will not marry the one with whom you are keeping company. To the aged, it is a sign of danger. 769

CHALK—To see a great deal of chalk, denotes great learning. 734

To eat chalk signifies a bad stomach, generally a burning in the stomach. 178

CHAMPAIGN—To dream of drinking champaign signifies that in the near future, you are going to eat the best, drink the best, wear the best and associate with some of the finest people in the world. 244

CHAMPION—To see one in your sleep denotes that you will be successful in the campaign that you are now conducting. 727

CHAPEL—To visit one is a sign of marriage followed by years of prosperity. 222

CHARACTER—To dream that your conduct is being questioned denotes slander and deceit. 138

To dream that you are being praised, denotes popularity. 893

CHARCOAL—To dream of charcoal, denotes that some one is taking news about you to your wife or

husband. Be careful with the one, whom you
think is your best friend, for that person is a
news carrier. **395**

CHARIOT—To dream of going to heaven in a chariot,
denotes long life and prosperity. You should stop
worrying about death, as this dream indicates that
you will be here on this earth for a long time. **204**

CHARITY—To dream that you give alms to any one,
denotes a peaceful mind. It also indicates popularity. **536**

CHARLESTON—To dream of this dance denotes success and much happiness. **205**

CHECK—To dream of a check denotes that you will
lose a small amount of money. **118**

CHEMISE—If a man dreams of seeing his sweetheart
in a short chemise, it is a sign of unfaithfulness.
She is in love with someone else. **719**

CHEMIST—To dream of one denotes that you will
change your condition and present surroundings.
346

CHEMISTRY—To dream of the science of chemistry
indicates that you will obtain a good paying position shortly. **671**

CHEESE—To dream of a large cheese denotes that
you will succeed in executing your plans in ac-
cordance with your wishes. Things are going to
work out to suit you. **167**

CHEESE-CLOTH—To dream of cheese-cloth signifies
that you will be having a set of beautiful furniture shortly. **394**

CHERRY—To dream of ripe cherries denote sudden
wealth. **185**

Young cherries denote sickness and vexation. **935**

CHEWING GUM—To dream of chewing gum, de-
noted that some one is going to borrow a sum
of money from you. Do not lend your money to
that person. If you do, you will lose it. **217**

CHICKENS—To dream of chickens signify that you are about to undertake a prosperous and significant adventure. **183**

CHILDREN—To see many children denotes that some of your children will become school teachers. One of them will become a principal, and be active in educational circles. **212**

CHIMNEY—To see smoke coming from a chimney, signifies that you will receive a nice present from your darling. **183**

CHINAMAN—To dream of one, denotes sudden wealth and good health. **122**

CHINESE—To see a chinese is a sign of wealth, happiness and the picture of good health. **731**

CHIROPODIST—To have one attend you signifies a pleasant trip. **114**

CHIROPRACTOR—To see one in your sleep denotes that you will enjoy the blessings of peace and prosperity, for which you had long hoped. **297**

CHISEL—To dream of one denotes that you have a very sharp temper. This dream warns you to control your fiery temper a little more. **714**

CHLOROFORM—To dream of taking chloroform signifies that you will cause a little trouble to a friend. For this deed you are going to regret. **511**

CHOIR—To hear them sing signifies joy and profit. **318**
To dream that you join the choir, portrays a peaceful existence. **638**

CHOP-SUEY—To dream of this luxury for the stomach, signifies a great deal of enjoyment among friends. **419**

CHRISTENING—Signifies that you are well versed in human frailities. **312**

CHURCH—Signifies a prosperous and happy life. **269**

CHURCH-YARD—Signifies mourning, and the loss of a friend, or a relative. **362**

CHRISTMAS—To dream of Christmas is a sign of joy and happiness in abundance. It denotes that all of your troubles are over. You can now look forward to peace and prosperity until the end of times. 231

CIDER—Denotes sudden joy. 943

CIGAR—Foretells that you will succeed to a remarkable degree. 870

CIGARETTE—To dream of a cigar, denotes that you are going to catch a cold by not dressing yourself warm enough. 344

CINNAMON—To see it denotes courage and security in business. 321

CIRCUS—To dream of a circus, denotes that you are going to have new experience. 447

CIVIL SERVICE—To dream of taking a civil service examination indicates that you are going to get a better position than the one you have. 173

CLEARING HOUSE—To dream of the Clearing House signifies an abundance of money. You are going to be lucky in games of chances. This is an excellent dream to all, especially to the needy. 716

CLIFF—To dream of a cliff signifies strange adventures. 521
To fall from a cliff denotes that if you do not exercise judgment you will lose some money by wild cat investment. 526

CLIMB—To climb a hill denotes success. To dream that you are unable to reach the hill denotes failure in your undertakings. 182

CLOCK—To dream of a clock. denotes steady and profitable employment. 769

CLOG—A wooden clog denotes that your ways are too ancient. This warns you to adopt modern ideas. 462

CLOTHES—New clothes denotes happiness. 369
Old clothes is a sign of failure. 598

CLOUDS—Clear clouds denote a brilliant future. 900 Dark clouds denote failure. You should therefore abandon your present plans. 832

CLOVER—Clover denotes riches. This is a very good dream for people in all walks of life. 229

CLOWN—To see one in your sleep denotes pleasure and happiness. 431

COACH—To ride in one, signifies sudden joy. 426

COALS—To dream of coals, signify want and sufferings. 316

COCOA—To dream of cocoa signifies a happy and a prosperous life; enjoyment among friends and relatives. 536

COCOANUT—Denotes that you will inherit a large sum of money and other property at the death of a relative. 527

CODFISH—To dream of codfish signifies weakness on your part to do what is right, to carry out your plans successfully. 144

COFFEE—To dream that you drink a cup of coffee, signifies warmth and protection. 167

COFFIN—To see one denotes sad news from afar. 183

COLLAR—To dream of one denotes that you are going to get a decent position. You will be well dressed at all times. 324

COLLEGE—To visit one is a sign of happiness. 690 To dream that you are a college student denotes popularity. 369

COLORED PEOPLE—To dream of colored people denote that you will become comfortably rich in the near future. 752

COMBING HAIR—Denotes clever business transactions. 181

COMPASS—To dream of a compass, signifies that you will go through life successfully. 791

CONCERT—To dream of a concert is a sign of matrimony. It also promises much happiness. **341**

CONCRETE—To dream of concrete, indicates that you are going to be the owner of a beautiful cottage shortly. This cottage will have a large garage. It will be surrounded by beautiful gardens. The location of this house will be one of civic beauty. **734**

CONCUBINES—Denotes a bad plague. **531**

CONFESSION—To dream that you make a confession of any act, signifies that you will commit an act of indecency, only to show off on your friends. **193**

CONSERVATORY—To dream of a conservatory, denotes that in the near future you will become very prominent in school circles. To a man he will be a man among men. To a woman she will be a woman among women. **131**

CONSPIRACY—To enter one, is a sign of business success and elaborate expansion. **549**

CONTEST—To enter a contest signifies, that you are a keen observer of human frailities. This indicates that you are of a tender, and lovable disposition with a keen interest for the unfortunate. **321**

CONTRACT—To dream of making a contract, signifies that you will have connection with a shrewd business person. **534**

COOK—To dream of cooking indicates that some one is trying to live at your expense. That person has more money than you, but that individual is only trying to be smart. **326**

COOK-BOOK—To dream of one signifies an important engagement will be broken by you. **414**

CORK—Denotes profitable employment of long duration. **973**

CORK SCREW—To dream of a cork screw, denotes that you will have a hard time in collecting the money that is due to you. **182**

CORN MEAL—To dream of corn meal denotes fairly good circumstances. **538**

CORONET—This dream denotes that you will receive good news in a very short time. **215**

CORONATION—To dream of one, signifies good luck in games of chances. **387**

CORPSE—To see one denotes a marriage shortly. **152**

CORRESPONDENCE—Denotes business difficulties for a while. **501**

COTTON—To dream of cotton, signifies poverty and vexation of spirit. It also denotes that your earning capacity is decreasing. **384**

COURT HOUSE—To see one in your sleep denotes secret enemies. **775**

COUSIN—To dream of your cousin, denotes steady employment for a few years. **763**

COWBOY—To dream of one denotes benevolence. **596**

COWS—To see them grazing signify a happy and prosperous life. To milk them, denotes wealth and happiness. **705**

CRAB—To see one in your sleep denotes that you will receive a sum of money shortly. With this money you are going to make more money and you will therefore become a leader in politics in your community. **845**

CRADLE—Denotes that you will have a baby girl. To a man his wife loves him with all her heart and soul. **371**

CRANBERRIES—Denote a peaceful mind. **292**

CRANBERRY SAUCE—Denotes joy and profit. **367**

CRAZY—To dream of a crazy person is a sign of sudden wealth. **085**

CREAM—To dream of using cream, denotes that your wife, husband or sweetheart is sincere. **184**

CREDITORS—To dream of them denotes peace and

prosperity. **331**

CREOLE—Signifies sudden joy and prosperity. **365**

CRICKETING—To see this game is a sign of prosperity and good health. **100**

CRIPPLE—To see a cripple person in your sleep, denotes sad news. **342**

CROCODILE—To dream of a crocodile, denotes that you will discover a secret. **121**

CROWN—Foretells a good paying position. **919**

CRYING—To dream of crying, denotes great joy **734**

CUP—A filled cup denotes sudden wealth. **524**
   An empty cup signifies fairly good circumstances. **365**

CURTAINS—Signify that your business will improve gradually, and that you will recover your losses. **119**

CUSHION—To see one in your scleep, denotes that you will be having an elaborate furnished home shortly. Your house is going to be the talk of the town. You will be having swell rugs and some of the finest draperies they are in the country. **121**

CUSTOM HOUSE—Is a sign of travel and adventure. It also indicates a peaceful mind. **318**

CUT—To dream of cutting yourself is a sign of dis content and destruction of your plans. **518**

CUTTING CORNS—Denotes health and prosperity To cut the corn of others is a sign of failure. **219**

CYLINDER—To see one in motion denotes a brilliant future. **718**
   If the cylinder is at a standstill, it indicates that you will have a slow season this year. **817**

DAFFODILS—Denote sadness of short duration. **825**

DAGGGER—To dream of a dagger, denotes that you will go through some strange experiences. **761**
   To stab any one with a dagger, signifies that you will triumph over your enemies. **412**

DAIRY—Is a sure sign of prosperity throughout the succeeding years of your life. **361**

DAIRY-MAID—To see one in your sleep, signifies that you will be married shortly. **572**

DAISY—To dream of this flower is a sign of good fortune in all games of chances and other speculations. **956**

DAMAGE SUIT—To dream that you bring a damage suit against any one signifies that you are being robbed out of your labor. **253**

To dream that a damage suit is brought against you, signifies a little embarrassment. **321**

DAME—To see a pretty girl in your sleep denotes immediate success and a happy ending of all your troubles. **401**

To kiss a pretty dame, denotes that you will be the recipient of divine kisses and caresses from your sweetheart. **310**

DAMSEL—To dream of a good looking damsel denotes joy to your heart's content. It also signifies peace and an abundance of everlasting happiness. **119**

DANCE—To dream that you dance is a sign of joy and perpetual happiness. **213**

To dream that you attend a dance, but do not dance is a sign of discontent. **469**

DANDELION—Denotes a marked and successful career. **660**

DANDRUFF—To dream that your head is covered with dandruff, is a sign of wealth and happiness. **226**

DANGER—To be in danger denotes anger and disillusion. **605**

DARKNESS—To dream of darkness, denotes that your eyes need medical care. You should wear glasses. **614**

DARNING—Denotes health and much prosperity. **391**

DARNING STOCKINGS—Denotes domestic happiness. **631**

DATES—To eat them denote joy and profit. To turn away from them, losses. To give them away signify domestic tranquility. **406**

DAVENPORT—To dream that you sit or sleep in a davenport, denotes a peaceful mind. It also indicates that you will triumph over your enemies. regardless of conditions. **173**

DEACON—To dream of a deacon signifies that you are about to become an active member of some religious and patriotic organization. **632**

To quarrel with a deacon denotes persecuton. **385**

DEAD—To dream of a dead, denotes mischief from an unexpected source. **679**

To talk to dead persons mark their words carefully. **239**

DEARTH—Denotes good crops to the farmers. To others it indicates that you will receive a sum of money shortly. **799**

DEAF—To talk to a deaf person, denotes that you should make use of your past experience, and therefore be benefited in transacting and dealing with your present and future problems, whether they be small or great, because small problems grow by leaps and bounds. **263**

DEATH-BED—To be present at a death-bed denotes that you will be melancholy for a little time. **223**

DEBATE—To enter into a debating contest signifies that you will become very popular in your community through your steadfastness of purpose. **596**

To dream of a debating organization, signifies long life and happiness. **963**

DECEITFUL PERSON—To dream of a deceitful person, denotes that your enemies are more than a match for you. **363**

DECIMAL—To dream of decimal fractions is a sign of

bearing false witness against your neighbor. **011**

DECORATE—To dream of having your room decorated signifies that you will succeed in executing all of your plans. **217**

DECORATION DAY—To dream of this day denotes everlasting security and happiness. **218**

DEER—Denotes a sad and lonesome life. To kill one is a sign of sad news. **414**

DELEGATE—To dream of any kind of a delegate, signifies that you will receive an increase in salary. **411**

To quarrel with one, denotes lost hope. **457**

DELICATESSEN—To see one denotes that you will over eat. **891**

DEMOCRATIC—To dream of the democratic party, denotes business success. **736**

DEMONSTRATION—To dream of a demonstration denotes that you will rise far above your present position and be happy, throughout the succeeding years of your life. **613**

DEN OF THIEVES—To be caught by a den of thieves denotes that the prisoner will receive a suspended sentence. **316**

DENTIST—To dream of one signifies pain and misery of short duration. **634**

DEPORTATION—To dream of a deportation, denotes loss and unhappiness. **171**

DEPUTY—To dream of one denotes law suits in which you will win. **727**

DERRICK—To see one in your sleep, denotes hard work, but good pay. **181**

DESERT—To dream of being in a desert denotes a sorrowful life. **101**

DESERTER—To dream of a deserter, denotes that you will lose a small amount of money, generally by gambling or such like. **142**

DESSERT—To partake of dessert is a sign of good

fortune. **261**

DESIGNER—To dream of a designer, denotes that
you will have a beautiful, well furnished home
shortly. **324**

DESPONDENCE—To dream of being despondent
signifies the reverse in business. **394**

DESTITUTE—To see a destitute person in your
sleep denotes that you will meet with keen com-
petition in your business or occupation **639**

DETECTIVE—To dream of a detective, denotes that
you will be protected by one in power. **213**

DEVIL—To see this destroyer of man's hope is a
sign of dissatisfaction. **182**
To overthrow this fellow, or chase him away, signifies that you will triumph over your enemies. **832**

DEW—To dream of the dew signifies that you will
now enjoy the blessing of peace and prosperity,
for which you had long hoped. Everything is now
in your favor. Whatever you do will be blessed,
for success is falling upon you like the gentle
drops of dew from heaven. **632**

DIAGRAM—To dream of any kind of a diagram,
signifies that the plans you have laid out are correct, proceed and put them into action at once.
Do not delay. **191**

DIALOGUE—To recite one is a sign of wealth and
popularity. **533**

DIAMOND—To dream of a diamond, denotes that
your employer is more than pleased with the way
in which you go about your daily task. You will
receive an increase in salary shortly. **423**

DIARRHEA—Denotes a change of address shortly.
To see others afflicted with this sickness, foretells
a great deal of pleasure. **674**

DICE—To dream of dice signifies, that you will have
a misunderstanding among friends or relatives. **711**
To win at dice signifies pleasure. **217**

DICTIONARY—To dream of a dictionary signifies that through your clean way of living, you will be called upon to give advice to some poor unfortunate person. **129**

DIGGING—To dream of digging anything, signifies that you will discover a startling secret. **118**

DINING-ROOM—To dream of sitting in a dining room signifies that you will receive a declaration of love from your sweetheart. **324**

To see others sitting in a dining room indicate that you will be honored by a person of high caste. **415**

DINNER—This dream indicates a brilliant future. **346**

DIPLOMA—To receive one signifies that you will be elevated to a higher position in life through your own skill. **273**

DISABLE—To dream that you are disabled is a sign of reform. You should, therefore, look on the brighter side of life. **319**

To see others disabled denotes a successful career. **742**

DISASTER—To dream of a catastrophe, denotes danger from an unexpected source. **381**

DISCONTENT—Denotes an increase in salary. **708**

DISCOURAGED—To dream of being discouraged in your sleep is a sure sign of sadness. It indicates lost hopes. **121**

DISEASE—Denotes that you are wasting money and time on someone who does not appreciate your hospitality. **932**

DISGRACE—To dream of being disgraced denotes popularity, and success. **616**

DISGUISED—To dream that you disguise yourself, denotes that some one in whom you have much confidence will betray you. **213**

To see a disguised person, denotes that you will know the truth about a peculiar affair. **367**

DISHES—To dream of clean dishes is a sign of wealth

Dirty dishes denote poverty and remorse. **272**

DISHONEST—To dream of a dishonest person is a sign of temptation. **922**

DISOBEDIENCE—To dream of being disobedient denotes a successful career. **600**

DISPENSARY—To dream of a dispensary is a sign of wealth, health and happiness. **311**

DIPHTERIA—Denotes sadness and contempt. **840**

DISPOSSESS—To dream that you are dispossessed denotes petty quarrels. **711**

DISTILLERY—To see one in your sleep is a sign of pleasure and excessive drinking among friends. **341**

DITCH—To dig one denotes small profits. To fall into one denotes shame. To see others fall into a ditch denotes that you will rise to higher position in your community and you will be very happy. **567**

DIVING BELT—Denotes joy and profit. **871**

DIVORCE—To dream of a divorce case, denotes notoriety. **223**
To dream that you are suing for a divorce is a sign of popularity among prominent people. **361**

DOCK—To dream you are at the dock signifies that your friends or relatives will have a pleasant trip. **334**
To see many ships at the dock, denotes a brilliant and eventful future. **433**

DOCTOR—To see one denotes gain. To have one attend you is a sign of domestic tranquility. **215**

DOCUMENTS—To see any kind of documents in your sleep signifies a happy life. **182**

DOG—To see a black dog denotes a dangerous adventure, but nevertheless you will be successful. **371**
If the dog bites you, it denotes loss. **511**
To run away from a dog is a sign of domestic hap-

piness. **194**

A white dog is a sign of sudden wealth. **371**

A Police dog, denotes that you will overcome your enemies. **441**

To see many dogs, denote that you will be successful in winning your case. It warns you to summons all of your witnesses in order to prove your point. **154**

DOUGHNUTS—To eat them denote profit. To turn away from them is a sign of unhappiness. **364**

DOVE—To dream of a dove denotes that you will be admired by all. You will receive the milk of human kindness. **815**

To see many doves signify that your engagement is one of reality. Your sweet-heart loves you dearly and he means good towards you. **158**

DRAPERIES—To dream of draperies. signifies that your home will be elaborately furnished in the near future. It will be the talk of the town. **659**

DRAWING ROOM—To sit in your drawing room denotes that some one is trying to wreck the happiness between you, and your sweetheart. **674**

To see others sitting in your living room denotes that your wife or sweetheart is unfaithful. **417**

DRESS—To dream of a white dress, denotes that you are a person of extraordinary sagacity. You have a keen perception of life in general. **293**

A black dress signifies that you will mourn for a little while, generally for a friend. **152**

A silk dress denotes long life and happiness. **736**

A Pink dress denotes love and joy to your heart content. **716**

DRSSSING GOWN—To dream of a dressing gown, denotes tender and loving affection. It indicates that your wife or husband is true to you. **184**

DRINKS—To dream of a variety of drinks signify sudden wealth. **333**

DRIVE—To dream that you take long drives, denotes

that some one is in love with you. It also indicates that you are at peace with the world. **346**

DRUG STORE—To see one, signifies that the sick will recover, because you are now using the right remedy. **767**

DRUGGIST—To see one in yor sleep, denotes that one of your friends is broken in health. **515**

DRUM—To hear one beat, denotes that you triumph over your enemies. **734**

DRUNK—To dream of being drunk denotes misery. **563**

To see others drunk denotes luck in games of chances. **711**

DUCK—To dream of a duck, signifies that you will travel by water shortly. This trip will be one of great success. **726**

DUET—To dream of a duet denotes that you will become a great musician. **144**

DUGOUT—To see one in your sleep denotes adversity. **321**

DUMB WAITER—To dream of one signifies a happy and prosperous marriage. Your life will be filled with sunshine, and much happiness. You will be able to eat the best, drink the best, and wear the very best. **495**

DUNGEON—To be confined in one, denotes secret sorrows. **421**

To see one, but not enter it, is a sign that you will catch some one stealing from you. **137**

DUPE—To dream of dupe denotes that you are wasting valuable time. **123**

DUPE FIEND—To see one in your sleep, denotes that you are making more of a certain person than you should. That person does not deserve so much praise, especially from you. You are too kind hearted in that respect. **634**

DYING—To dream of a dying person indicates profitable investments. **398**

DYE—To dream of any kind of a dye, denotes that you will change your mode of living shortly. You will be benefitted by the change, for it will not only bring you health, but also an abundance of wealth. **391**

DYNAMITE—To dream of dynamite denotes danger from an unexpected source. Your plans will be disorganized. **161**

EAGLE—To dream of an eagle denotes sudden wealth. **146**

To see many eagles, denote that you will have many dutiful and loving children, three boys and two girls. **649**

EARS—To dream that your ears are larger than usual signify that you will discover a startling secret. **328**

To dream that they have grown smaller clearly indicates that you will never be able to solve the problem in which you are now interested. **327**

EAR RINGS—To see them in your sleep signify peace and much happiness. It is truly a sign of prosperity. **871**

To see others wearing ear rings is a sign of much enjoyment and satisfaction. **870**

EARTHEN-WARE—To dream of earthen-ware is a sign of good luck on the following day. It also indicates a loving husband, wife or sweetheart. **169**

EARTH-QUAKE—To dream of earth-quake, signifies danger from an unexpected source. **327**

EARTH-WORM—Denotes good luck in all games of chances. **671**

To kill an earth-worm is a sign of misunderstanding among friends or relatives. **923**

EASTER—To dream of this holiday, denotes joy and much happiness. It also indicates that you will have nice clothes shortly for which you had long hoped. **187**

ECLIPSE—To witness one is a warning of reform. If you adhere to this dreaf, you will certainly succeed in executing all of your plans. **418**

EDDOES—Denotes shrewd business transactions. To see them grow is a sign of love and affection. To reap them indicates a brilliant future. **691**

EDUCATION—To pursue an education is a sign of great intelligence and security in all kinds of business. To see others interested in learning indicate luck in games of chances. **741**

EGGS—To dream of eggs indicate joy and much profit. **273**

Broken eggs denote slander and jealousy. **091**

EGG PHOSPHATE—To drink it is a sign of slander from one who is far below your social standing. **881**

ELBOW—Denotes that you possess a pleasing personality. It also indicates good health accompanied by much prosperity. **831**

ELECTION—To dream of an election, denotes that you should find no time, searching for nothing to do. **234**

ELECTRIC METER—Denotes a profitable investment. which will be attributed to your keen judgment and adaptability. To read one indicates wisdom. **660**

ELECTRICIAN—To see one in your sleep, signifies that you will move to better quarters shortly. It also indicates that you will become very prominent in your community and as a result. you will be very happy. **265**

ELECTRICITY—To dream of electricity, denotes gratified ambition. **174**

ELEPHANT—To dream of an elephant, denotes power and dignity. It further indicates that you will succeed well in life. **739**

ELEVATOR—To ride in one denotes great business enterprises. It is a sign of gradual wealth and happiness. **637**

ELK—To dream of the order of Elks denotes prosperity and happiness. To dream that you are inducted in this order indicates that you are highly intellectual, and on account of your wit, you will succeed in executing your present plans. **285**

ELM TREE—To see one in your sleep denotes a happy and prosperous life. This is a very pleasant dream to all, since it promises security in all kinds of business. **710**

ELOCUTION—To dream of studying elocution is a sign of a speedy and prosperous marriage. **615**

ELOPE—To dream that you elope with the one you love is a sign of joy and much happiness followed by years of prosperity. To old people it indicates that they are becoming more religious as the years roll on. **109**

ELOQUENT—To dream of an eloquent person, indicates, that you are a person of extraordinary sagacity. **625**

EMBALMING—To witness one signifies trouble and vexation of spirit. To dream that you are an embalmer denotes temptation. Control yourself. **327**

EMBARRASS—To dream that you are in an embarrassing position indicates that some of your friends will try to frame you, but they will be unsuccessful in their effort. **125**

EMBLEM OF LOVE—To receive a declaration of love from your sweetheart is a sign of excessive pleasure. It also indicates a happy and prosperous life. It is a sign of courage and steadfastness of purpose. **911**

EMBRACE—To dream that you are being embraced by one who loves you, signifies a peaceful and

happy existence. It also indicates a loving wife
husband or sweetheart. **633**

EMBROIDERY—Is a sign of domestic tranquility.
It also indicates love affairs. **611**

EMERALD—Signifies a happy and prosperous life.
273

EMIGRANTS—Denote that you will become very
prosperous and happy in your community. This
is due to your popularity in the vicinity. **200**

EMINENT MEN—To see them in your sleep is a
sign of great intelligence and ample ability in
executing your plans. **474**

EMPEROR—To dream of one signifies honor and dignity. It is also a sign of good health and wealth.
760

EMPLOYMENT—To dream that you receive employment is a sign of prosperity and health. It also
indicates that you will obtain and control large
sums of money in the near future. **651**

EMPLOYMENT AGENCY—Signifies the loss of your
present position. **317**
To see others in an employment agency is a sign of
power and much prosperity. **367**

EMPLOYER—To dream of your employer, signifies
that you will overcome your present obstacle. **237**

ENDORSE—To dream that you endorse a note denotes that you will become a prominent business
person. **182**
To endorse a note as co-maker, denotes losses. **782**

ENGAGEMENT—To dream that you break an engagement, denotes that you are not a trust worthy person. It clearly indicates that you are fickle minded
773

ENGINEER—To dream of one is a sign of will power.
It indicates that you will become very prosperous
in the near future. **613**

ENEMY—To dream of your enemy is a sign of grief

It also indicates secret sorrows. **327**

If however, you defeat your enemy, it denotes joy and profit. **311**

ENGRAVER—Denotes that you are about to have your photographs taken. **217**

ENJOYMENT—To dream that you enjoy yourself among friends, denotes that you will accomplish the task which you now have in your mind. **394**

ENRAGE—To dream that you get into a rage, signifies that you will hear something which will upset you for a little while. **771**

ENVELOPE—To dream of an empty envelope, denotes that you will be the recipient of news which you do not wish to hear. **319**

ENVY—To dream that you are being envied denotes that you will become more prosperous as the years roll on. **632**

EPIDEMIC—To dream of an epidemic, denotes hardship of short duration. **271**

EQUATOR—To visit the equator is a sign of health and great wealth. **116**

ESCAPE—To dream that you escape from a confinement, signifies that you will outwit your enemies at their own game. **315**

ESCORT—To dream of having an escort signifies that you are well protected. **184**

To quarrel or chase away your escort is a sign of danger. To married people, it indicates divorce proceeding. **461**

ESSAY—To read or write an essay, signifies that you will rise far above your present position and that you will be happy throughout the years to come. **347**

ETHIOPIAN—To dream of one is a sign of wealth and much happiness. To quarrel with one, denotes loss of goods by fire or robbery. **361**

ETIQUETTE—To read the rules of etiquette is a sign

that you are about to crash into society and become very popular. **911**

EUROPEAN—To see one in your sleep, denotes economic slavery. To quarrel with one denotes losses. **316**

EVANGELIST—To dream of an evangelist, signifies a peaceful, loving wife or sweetheart. **187**

EVIDENCE—To dream of giving evidence, is a sign of misunderstanding among friends or relatives. **174**

EXAMINATION—To dream of taking or going through any kind of examinations, is sign of benevolence and satisfaction. **401**

EXCHANGE OFFICE—Denotes that you will fall heir to a large sum of money shortly. It also indicates extensive travel and adventure. **321**

EXCURSION—To dream of going on an excursion, signifies that you will marry your present lover. It also indicates that your life will be filled with sunshine and happiness. **003**

EXCUSE—To dream of making an excuse, signifies, that you will tell a lie, in order to shield a dear friend. **224**

EXECUTIONEER—To see one in your sleep, signifies an unfortunate investment. **327**

EXHAUST—To dream that you become exhausted from a journey, denotes great experience. **294**

EXHIBITION—To dream of an exhibition is a sign of permanent employment, generally a government position. **087**

EXPLOSION—To dream of an explosion, denotes sudden wealth, generally a large sum of money. **036**

EXPOSE—To dream that you expose yourself is a sign of shame and remorse. **139**

EXPOSITION—To see one denotes an increase of knowledge. It also indicates prosperity and long life. **925**

EXPRESS—To dream of riding on an express train, denotes a change of address for the better. **634**

EYES—To dream that your eyes have grown larger, signify that you are a sympathetic person. It indicates that you have a keen perception of life, and that you are familiar with human weakness. **963**

To dream that your eyes have grown smaller, indicate small profits. **289**

EYE WASH—To dream of an eye wash, signifies that you need more ambition in order to carry out your plans. **121**

FACE—To dream that some one make funny faces at you, is a sign of mockery and shame. **257**

To dream that your face has grown larger is a sign of distress. **372**

FAIL—To dream that you fail in carrying out any of your plans, is a warning of reform. This dream indicates that you should change your mode of living in order to be sucecssful. **324**

FAINT—To see a person faint, denotes that you are a smart person. You are very intellectual, and for this reason you will succeed in all of your undertakings regardless of present or previous conditions. **611**

FAIRY—To dream of a fairy is a sign of joy, and much profit, followed by years of prosperity. **127**

FAIRYLAND—To dream that you visit a fairyland denotes an abundance of pleasure. It also indicates sudden wealth. **192**

FAITHFUL—To dream of being faithful is a sign of peace and consolation. **929**

FAKER—To dream of a faker is a sign of losses, which will be the direct result of your inexperience in transacting a certain business. **372**

FALL—To dream that you fall, signifies that you are going to make a mistake, which will not be very serious; but it will however, result in a loss to you. **735**

FALLEN ARCHES—This dream denotes that the prisoner will be released immediately. **990**

FALSEHOOD—This dream warns you to be careful in your conduct, or otherwise, you are liable to be framed, which as a result would cost you grave difficulty and inconvenience. **665**

FANCIFUL—To dream of being fantastic is a sign of love and romance to a remarkable degree. **210**

FAN—To dream of a fan is a sign of comfort. This dream clearly indicates that you will rise far above your present position and be happy. **141**

FAN DANCER—To see one in your sleep denotes an abundance of pleasure and good fortune. **936**

FAME—To dream that you become famous, signifies long life and much happiness accompanied by the picture of good health. **756**

FAMINE—To dream of a famine is a sign of troubled conscience. This dream warns you not to hold the secret any longer. **339**

FAREWELL PARTY—To dream that you give a farewell party, denotes that you will marry a wealthy person. Through this marriage you will become prominent in society. **159**

FARINA—This is indeed an excellent dream to farmers, as it indicates good crops; to others it is a sign of good fortune. **567**

FARM—To dream of a farm, denotes hard work but good pay. It also indicates that your present position is secure. **444**

FARMER—To dream of a farmer denotes that you will travel shortly. The trip will be one of great pleasure. **235**
To dream that you are a farmer, signifies that you will live comfortable and in good circumstances, but that you will never be rich. **039**

FARM HOUSE—Denotes the speedy return of your sweetheart. It also indicates divine love and caresses. **891**

FASHION—To dream of wearing the latest fashion denotes social ambition. It also denotes success in love affairs. **721**

FASTING—To dream of fasting is a sign of misfortune and great loss. It is truly a sign of disappointment. **740**

FATHER—To dream of your father is a very good sign to policy players. It indicates that you will win a sum of money in games of chances. **671**

FATHER-IN-LAW—To dream of your father-in-law, denotes that one of your so called friends is jealous of you. **718**

FATIGUE—To dream of being fatigued, denotes that you will receive a visit from a talkative person. This person thinks the world of you, although you will not appreciate this party, on account of the fact, that this person talks too much. **711**

FAT PERSON—To dream of a fat person, denotes joy and much profit. **160**

FAUCET—To dream of a faucet, indicates that you will remove from your present abode. The change will be to your utmost satisfaction. **213**
To dream that you are unable to obtain water from the faucet is a sign of poor business transaction on the following day. **721**

FEAST—To dream of a feast, signifies that you will be married shortly, to a person of wealth and position. **745**

FEATHERS—To dream of an abundance of feathers, denote that you will lead a successful life from now on, and that you will be happy through the coming years. **110**

FEET—To dream of having large feet, signify that you will travel a great distance suddenly. **219**

FENCE—To dream of a fence denotes protection. It also indicates a peaceful life. **256**

FERMENTATION—To dream of seeing any liquid ferment, signifies that you will become a celebrated bootlegger. From this business you will realize a decent sum of money. **117**

FERRYBOAT—To dream that you ride in a ferryboat, denotes that you will work a great distance away from home. This work will prove to be very advantageous to you. **745**

FEVER—To dream of having an attack of fever denotes, that you should take care of yourself more than you do at present. **530**

FIDDLE—To dream of a fiddle, denotes that you will form the acquaintance of a wealthy person. This person will look out for you financially. **233**

FIDDLER—To dream of a fiddler, signifies that you will be in low circumstances for a short time. You will be very successful next year. **365**

FIELD—To see a large field denotes that you will own and control a great deal of real estate in the near future. **794**

FIGHT—To dream of engaging in a fight, denotes that your neighbors envy you a great deal, on account of your success. Beware of them. Do not let your right hand know, what your left hand is doing. **391**

FILTH—To dream of filth denotes suden wealth. This is an excellent dream for those who try their luck in games of chances. **339**

FINGER—To dream of having an enormous large finger is a sign of wealth, and good health. **155**

FIRE—To dream of a fire denotes petty quarrels among friends and relatives. **324**

FIRE-ARM—To dream about any kind of a fire arm, signifies danger from an unexpected source. **169**

FIRE ENGINE—To dream of a fire engine, denotes

that you will receive a large sum of insurance money. **731**

FIREMAN—To dream of a fireman, signifies that you will be called upon to perform an honorable service which will be in the behalfs of humanity. **965**

FIRE FLY—Denotes that your partner is faithful and true to you in every respect. **969**

FIREPLACE—To see a bright burning fire in your fire hearth, denotes a brilliant future accompanied by the picture of good health. **316**

A dull fire, signifies slow progress on the part of the dreamer. **300**

FIRE WORKS—Foretells misery and shame. **601**

FISH—To dream of fish denote pregnancy to a woman. **267**

To a man a successful career providing that the fish are large. **387**

Small fish denote busness failure. **666**

FISHERMAN—To dream of a fisherman, denotes that you will succeed in obtaining the position that you are now seeking. **414**

FISHING—To dream that you go fishing, signifies that you will enter a good paying business. **293** To see others fishing denotes that you will go on a vacation shortly. **313**

FISH HOOK—This dream warns you that you will be outwitted by your enemies, unless you take great precautions in handling your present affairs. **670**

FIST—To dream of using your fist on any one, is a sign of your appearance before a court. **791**

FIT—To be afflicted with this sickness is a sign of failure. **116**

FLAG—To dream of a flag, denotes power and dignity. It also indicates long life and prosperity. **269**

FLAGSHIP—To see one signifies strife and vexation. **149**

FLAME—To see one burning brightly foretells a brilliant future; if dim, it is a sign of unhappiness. **418**

FLANNEL—This is a very good dream to the poor. It promises warmth, food, and shelter. **963**

FLAP-JACKS—Denote success in games of chances on the following day. **861**
To eat them signify popularity among friends and other associates. **840**

FLAT FOOT—To dream of having flat feet is a sign of cowardice. To see others with flat feet denote a change of residence for the better. **982**

FLEAS—Denote secret sorrows and troublesome enemies. **773**

FLIRT—To dream of flirting denotes that you will meet an infamous person. **021**

FLIRTING—To dream of flirting foretells that you are very cunning in your transactions. **371**
To see others flirting denote an abundance of pleasure. **139**

FLOATING—To see aything floating is a sign of wealth. **991**

FLORIST—Foretells peace and much prosperity. It also indicates that you are going to give a swell affair shortly. This party will be the talk of the town. **341**

FLOUR—Is a warning of reform. It also indicates that the prisoner will get a fair trial. He will be released within a few days. **619**

FLOWER—To dream of a flower, denotes that you will meet a person who will marry you providing you give your consent. **439**
A sweet smelling flower denotes an abundance of pleasure. **457**

FLUTE—To see one in your sleep, denotes a dreary life. **165**

To play one yourself denotes an increase in family, generally a baby boy. **736**

FLYING—To dream of flying, denotes an honorable and successful career. It promises long life and much happiness. This dream is of vital importance to the dreamer on account of the fact it clearly indicates so much prosperity. **723**

FLYING A KITE—Denotes good luck in all games of chances. This is a good dream to speculators **691**

FLYWHEEL—To see one in your sleep denotes a government position, which you will hold until you become too old, and then you will receive a pension. This is an excellent dream for those seeking employment, especially if you have a government position in mind. **373**

FOG—To dream that you are out in a fog signifies that you will outwit your enemies, and cause them a great deal of trouble. **346**

FOOD—To dream of an abundance of food, denotes that you will suffer from indigestion for a short time. You should therefore take warning, and not eat between meals. **332**

FOOTBALL—To play this game denotes success in all of your present undertakings. You need not have any fear. Go right ahead. **910**

FORECLOSURE—A foreclosure signifies hardship on the part of the dreamer. **347**

FOREST—To lose your way in a forest, is a sign of business difficulties. If however you are able to get out of the forest after having been lost for some time it indicates that you will recover your losses in a short time. **731**

FORGE—To see one in your sleep denotes hard work but good pay. **691**

FORGERY—Foretells disgrace and shame. **216**

FOREMAN—To dream of one is a sign of popularity **563**

　To dream that you are a foreman is a sign of riches. **691**

FORTUNE TELLER—To see one in your sleep, denotes that you will receive a legacy, left to you by a relative. **191**

FOUNDRY—To work in one signifies long life and some wealth. **064**

FOUNTAIN—Denotes a pleasant and happy vacation. **081**

　A soda fountain denotes security in business. **811**

FOUNTAIN PEN—To dream of a fountain pen denotes much prosperity. **151**

　To buy one denotes sudden joy. **635**

　To give one away foretells anxiety. **342**

　To lose one foretells that you will be worried for a while. **963**

FOWL—To dream of a fowl denotes a successful business career. **444**

FOX—Signifies an extremely cold winter but a lovely summer. **871**

FOX HUNTING—To dream of fox hunting denotes that you will lose confidence in one whom you believed, were very sincere to you. **664**

FRANKFURTER—Foretells laziness and slander. **522**

FRATERNITY—To dream of joining any fraternal order is a sign of riches and popularity. **741**

FRAUD—To dream of entering into any fraudulent business is a sign of disgrace. **323**

　To talk to a fraudulent person foretells immoralty **360**

FRECKLES—To dream of freckles denote riches in proportion to the number of freckles. **371**

FREEZE—To dream that it is freezing cold is a sign of protection to the poor. **251**

FREIGHT—To dream of freight train or boat, denotes success in commerce. **263**

FRESH WATER—To dream of fresh clear water, denotes wealth and happiness. **956**

FRIEND—To dream of a friend, denotes that you will form the acquaintance of a well trained person. **259**

FROG—To dream of a frog, signifies that you will have a great many children, all of whom will be highly educated, and as a result, they will hold prominent positions in the community. They will be doctors, lawyers, engineers and so forth. **291**

FRUITS—Ripe fruits denote success. **295**

Young fruits, signify misfortune and dissatisfaction. **002**

FRYING—Denotes peace and satisfaction, and the picture of good health.**716**

FRYING PAN—Denotes sudden wealth. **616**

FULL DRESS SUIT—To see a person in a full dress suit, denotes that you will attend an up-to-date social function. At this gathering you will meet some of the finest people in the community. **298**

FURS—To dream of furs signify that your sweetheart is faithful. **500**

FUNERAL—To dream of a funeral, signifies that you will receive a sum of money left you by a sincere friend or relative. **632**

FURNACE—To see a hot furnace, indicates want and suffering. **053**

A cold furnace, denotes prosperity. **182**

FURNITURE—To dream of new furniture signifies that you will move into better quarters shortly. It also indicates long life and happiness. **471**

Old furniture is a sign of losses by fire. **643**

GAIN—To dream of gaining anything legally, denotes a profitable enterprise. **183**

To gain anything by dishonest means, signifies a

law suit in which you will lose. **333**

GALE—To dream of a gale, denotes a misunderstand
ing among friends or relatives. **369**

GALLERY—To sit in your gallery foretells prosperity
and good health. It also denotes that you will receive a letter which will contain exceedingly good
news. **808**

GALLEY BIRD—Foretells a glorious adventure. **021**

GALLEY WORM—To see one denotes much happiness. **329**

To kill them denote grief and vexation. **931**

GALLON—To dream of measuring a gallon of any
kind of liquid, denotes that your future is assured.
You need not have any fear, for you will be exceedingly prosperous. **444**

GALLOWS—To see one in your sleep, denotes riches
by dishonest means. **481**

To see a person ascending a gallows is a sign of
misery and shame. **053**

GAMBLE—To gamble in your sleep denotes wealth
and prosperity. This is a good dream, since life
itself is a gamble. **781**

GAMBLER—Signify a profitable business enterprise.
625

GAME OF CARDS—To play a game of cards, denotes
that you will lead a comfortable life in the near
future, and that you will be prosperous through
out the succeeding years of your life. **510**

GANGSTER—To see one in your sleep is a warning
of reform. If you do not change your mode of
living, you will certainly come to a bitter end. **289**

GANGWAY—To walk up a gangway, denotes a pleasant trip. From this trip you will have experiences, which will help you a great deal in later
life. **961**

GARAGE—To dream of being in a garage is a sign
of owning an automobile. This dream indicates

long life and prosperity. **425**

GARBAGE—To see a great deal of garbage, denotes that you will meet a wolf in sheep's clothing. This means that you will meet a dishonest person who is after your money. Have nothing to do with this notorious character. If you do not mingle with this person, then you will marry the man or woman to whom you are now engaged. The marriage wil be one of great success. **193**

GARDEN—To walk in one signifies a pleasant surprise. **603**

To gather or admire flowers in a garden is a sign of domestic happiness accompanied by wealth. **938**

A poorly kept garden signifies slow progress in life. **456**

GARLIC—To see a great deal of garlic, denotes superstition. **185**

GARRISON—Signifies a prosperous and sedate life. **711**

GARTER—To dream of wearing garters, to a woman it denotes that a certain fellow is crazy about her. To a man it denotes that a certain girl loves him dearly. This is really a lovers dream. **164**

GARVEYISM—To dream of this doctrine foretells an honorable and successful career. **915**

GAS—To dream of gas denotes that you will own your own home shortly. **183**

GAS METER—To see one in your sleep, denotes that you will save a decent sum of money in the near future. With this money, you are going to open your own business. You will be successful in this particular line of business. **209**

GASOLINE—This dream indicates that you will have a new automobile in the near future. **206**

GATE—To see a heavy gate in your sleep denotes protection to the homeless, to others it signifies prosperity, regardless of present conditions. **144**

GATHERING—To see a large gathering, denotes that you are about to change your place of worship. **093**

GAZING—To dream of gazing at any one signifies that you are going to become very troublesome in your community, unless you change your ideas. **341**

GEMS—To dream of gems signifies sudden wealth. **012**

GENERAL—To see one in your sleep, denotes that you will rise far above your present position in life and be happy for the rest of your life. **267**

To dream that you quarrel with a general, denotes strife and vexation. **345**

GEOMETRY—To dream of the science of Geometry signifies gratified ambition. **129**

GERMAN—To see one in your sleep, denotes success in all of your undertakings. It also indicates that you are going to break down the social barrier and plunge into the limelight. **105**

GHOST—To see one in your sleep, denotes danger from an unexpected source. This dream warns you to be careful in transacting business, and your contact with people of questionable character. **257**

GIANT—To see one in your sleep denotes power and dignity, accomplished by your genius and learning. **163**

GIFT—To dream of giving away anything, signifies that you are a kind hearted person, for it is a pleasure to give, rather than to receive. The giver in many cases feels that he has rendered a great service, while the receiver, generally thinks he is obligated, or that he is receiving charity. **423**

GIN—To drink it denotes law suit. To give it away is a sign of success. **271**

To see others intoxicated with gin denotes loss. **215**

GINGER—To dream of ginger signifies that you are

friends are true. **191**

GINGERBREAD—Signifies good luck in games of chances on the following day. **361**

GIPSY—To dream of one mark her words, and do just what she says, except in the giving away of your money. Never give money away easily. Be sure that your money is well spent. **959**

GIRAFF—To dream of a giraffe, denotes that you will have a son, who will find a great deal of pleasure in hunting. **147**

GIRL—To dream of a young girl signifies that your friends are true. **191**

GLAD RAGS—To dream of dressing up in your best apparel denotes that you will go on an excursion shortly. **605**

GLASS—To drink from a glass signifies slight sickness. **112**
To spill water from a glass denotes that you are neglecting your business. **316**
To dream of a looking glass denotes that you will regain your health soon. **211**

GLOBE—To dream of a globe denotes that you will perform a great act in the behalfs of mankind. **651**

GLOVES—To wear them denotes luck on the following day. It signifies that your hopes will be realized. **831**

GOAT—To dream of a white goat, denotes prosperity. **725**
A white one is a sign of approaching marriage. **030**

GODCHILD—To dream of your godchild, to a young woman it denotes that she is pregnant. **317**
To a man it denotes that his wife will be delivered of a beautiful baby girl. **315**

GODFATHER—To see your godfather, denotes that you will inherit a little money in the near future. **379**

GODMOTHER—Mark her words in order to be successful in your present undertakings. **379**

GOGGLES—To dream of wearing goggles signify that you will become socially prominent in the near future. It also indicates that you will command a great deal of wealth. **423**

GOLD—To dream of gold denotes that a dead relative is going to give you a set of lucky numbers in your sleep. It is up to you now to realize your desire. **219**

GOLD FISH—To see a gold fish, indicates joy and much happiness. **307**
An abundance of gold fish, denote a happy ending of all your troubles. It also indicates good health. **347**

GOLD MINE—To visit one, denotes that you will invest in a good paying business. **427**
To work in one denotes poverty. **345**

GOLDSMITH—To dream of one, signifies that you will be the recipient of a costly gift from your sweetheart. This present will be prized above all other gifts, since it is given by one who loves you dearly. **763**

GOLD TEETH—Denote loss of health. **321**
To dream of losing them is a sign of disappointment. **311**

GOLF—To play golf signifies, that you will invest your money advantageously. **715**

GONG—To hear a gong rings, signifies a wedding anniversary. **456**

GOOD LUCK—To dream that you are lucky is a sign that you will meet with a little failure. **301**

GOOSE—To see one in your sleep indicates that your wife or husband is faithful. **187**

GORILLA—To dream of a gorilla, signifies that you will form the acquaintance of an ignorant person, an impossible creature. **241**

GOSPEL—To dream of preaching the gospel, denotes

that you are religiously inclined. **136**

GOULASH—To dream of goulash, signifies that you will suffer from indigestion in the not far distant future. **681**

GOVERNOR—To dream of a governor signifies an increase in wealth. **801**

GOVERNESS—To dream that you are a governess, signifies that you are tender, and loving. You are loved and respected by all on account of your fine qualities. **578**

GOWN—To dream of a gown signifies that you are going to acquire a new set of fine clothes. **214**

GRADE—To dream of crossing a grade, is a sign of impending danger. You should take care of yourself more than ever.

GRAFT—To dream of giving or receiving graft, is a sure sign that you will enter into a racketeering business, from which you will derive a large sum of money. **419**

GRAIN—To dream of a great deal of grain, signifies that you will become very prominent in your community. It also indicates that you will control a vast amount of real estate. **157**

GRAMMAR—To dream of reading or discussing grammar, signifies that you will be the author of a popular book or song. **942**

GRANDCHILD—To see your grandchild, denotes that the closing years of your life will be filled with sunshine and happiness. **273**

GRANDFATHER—To dream of your grandfather, signifies joy and profit. **719**

GRANDMOTHER—To dream of your grandmother mark her words, and do as she bids you. This is an excellent dream to lovers. **146**

GRAPES—Ripe grapes denote riches in abundance **345**

Young grapes denote misfortune and unhappiness. **630**

GRASS—To see grass, denotes that there will be death in the family shortly. **312**

Dried grass denotes lost hope. **469**

GRASSHOPPER—To dream of a grasshopper, signifies that you will travel a great deal in order to earn a livelihood. **189**

GRAVE—To visit a grave, denotes a lonesome, sorrowful life. **143**

To see many graves opened, is a sign of a storm or an earthquake. **343**

GRAVE DIGGER—To dream of one denotes sadness; generally the loss of a friend or relative. **125**

GREEDY PERSON—To talk to one, denotes that you are too proud. You should change your ways, otherwise you will bring about your own down fall. **163**

GREEN BACKS—To find one denotes good luck and much prosperity. **361**

To give one away is a sign of excessive pleasure. **268**

To find one denotes security and popularity. **567**

GREY HAIR—To dream of having grey hair is a sign of honor and splendor. To see others with grey hair denotes long life and prosperity. **320**

GRINDSTONE—To see one in your sleep, denotes hard work, but good pay. **365**

A broken grinding stone denotes grief and vexation. **367**

GRIPPE—To dream that you have an attack of the grippe, signifies that you are in the company of a person who has a contagious disease. **194**

GROANING—To dream of groaning signifies pleasure in abundance. **944**

To hear others groan is a sign of obscurity. **418**

GROCER—Denotes profit and loss. It also denotes the birth of a chield. **561**

GROUND—To dream of lying on the ground denotes that you will lose part of your savings by invest ment. **919**

GROVE—To walk through a grove is a sign of a happy and prosperous marriage with many beautiful children. **760**

GRUDGE—To dream that some one has a grudge against you, signifies that you are more than a match for your enemies. **271**

GUILLOTINE—Is a sign of anger and danger. **733**

GUINEA PIG—To dream of a guinea pig, warns you not to marry the person to whom you are now engaged. If you do, you will be sorry. There is another person who loves you and will marry you as soon as you break your former engagement. **196**

GUITAR—To hear one signifies that you are deep-in love. **213**

GUMBOIL—Denotes that you will suffer internal injuries. **654**

GUN—To dream of a gun denotes anger. **217**

GUNBOAT—To dream of a gunboat, signifies that you will be protected by powerful friends. They will give you any kind of aid. **421**

GUNMAN—To dream of a gunman, denotes a massacre. **155**

GUN POWDER—To dream of gunpowder, signifies a troubled spirit. You should tell the secret and be at ease, and at peace with the world. **211**

GUTTER—To dream of a gutter denotes that some of your so called friends will bring about your downfall. The secret that you had possessed should have been kept to yourself. It will be your fault. **117**

GYMNASIUM—To see one in your sleep, denotes

that you will succeeed in obtaining the information for which you had long hoped. **654**

HACK LICENSE—Denotes gain by dishonest means. **367**

HACKMAN—To dream of a hackman, signifies that you will not be rich, although you will be able to supply your daily wants at all times. **743**

To argue with one denotes that some one is trying to cheat you out of your savings. **643**

HAIL—To dream of hail, signifies a sad life. **321**

HAIR—To dream that your hair is long and curly is a sign of domestic happiness. **719**

Extra short hair is a sign of domestic worries. **733**

Disorderly hair is a sign of immorality. **322**

HAIRDRESSER—To have one dress your hair, denotes that you will be called upon to fill an important position. **477**

To dream that you are a hairdresser, signifies prosperity throughout the coming years. **229**

To argue with one denotes failure in your undertakings. **323**

HAIR LIP—Signifies that you will be the best dressed person in your community. **601**

HAIRY MONSTER—To dream of one signifies profit and experience. **387**

HALF MOON—To see one in your sleep denotes long life and prosperity. **277**

A full moon denotes sudden wealth. **777**

HAM—To eat it, denotes that you will receive an increase in salary **733**

To turn away from it, denotes secret sorrows. **139**

HAMBURGER STEAK—Signifies long life and prosperity. It is also a sign of approaching marriage. **542**

HAMMER—To dream of a hammer, signifies hard work, but that you will be well paid for your labor. **837**

HAMMOCK—To dream of a hammock, denotes that you will be comfortably rich. It also indicates that you will succeed in raising the money to pay your mortgage. **186**

HAND BAG—To dream of a beautiful hand bag denotes that you will receive a declaration of love from your sweetheart. **118**

HANDS—To dream of hairy hands, denote good fortune. **762**

Skinny hands, denote sickness. **569**

Strong hands, denote power and dignity. **939**

work. **805**

HASH—To eat hash in your sleep, denotes a successful carreer. **736**

To turn away from it, and not to eat it, denotes sorrow. **627**

HANDCUFFS—To dream of handcuffs, denote horror. **104**

If however, you are able to free yourself from handcuffs, you will triumph over your enemies, by beating them at their own game. **279**

HANDKERCHIEF—To dream of one signifies that you will marry the person who is now following you around. **263**

HANG—To see a person hang in your sleep, denotes lost hopes. **210**

HARE—Denotes that your friends will aid financially. **110**

To see one on the jump signifies gain. **510**

HARLOT—To see one denotes a sporty life. **135**

To quarrel with one, is a sign of approaching danger from an unexepected source. **555**

HARNESS—Denotes that you are underpaid for your

HARP—To dream of playing a harp, denotes a wedding. If not you, some dear friend or relative will be married within a few months. **205**

HAT—To dream of a new hat signifies that you will succeeed in obtaining your desire. **518**

To lose your hat signifies the loss of your present position. **318**

An old hat signifies quarrels. **638**

A Panama hat denotes gaiety and happiness. **581**

HATCHET—To dream of a hatchet, denotes that you will work in a dangerous place. Be careful. **259**

HATE—To dream of hating some one is a sign of dissatisfaction. **625**

To dream that you are being hated by another sig nifies honor and power. **212**

HAY—Denotes success in business. It also denotes long life and prosperity. **324**

A wagon filled with hay indicates a gay life. **321**

HEAD—To dream of having a large head denotes brilliance. A small head denotes deception. **561**

HEADACHE—To dream of a headache signifies, that a dear friend or relative is a little indisposed, and he is trying his best to locate you. **207**

HEALTH—Signifies joy and much prosperity. **433**

HEART—A strong heart signifies health and wealth. A weak heart is a sign of approaching sickness. **264**

HEAT—To dream of extreme heat, denotes that you are going to visit a so called friend, your presence will not be appreciated. **411**

HEAVEN—To dream of going to heaven signifies a prosperous and glorious life. This is a nexcellent dream. **221**

HEIR—To dream that you fall heir to an inheritance denotes joy and long life, accompanied by extremely good health. **268**

HEMORRHAGE—To dream of having an attack of hemorrhage denotes anxiety and remorse. **219**

HERBS—To dream of herbs, signifies that you will invest in a good paying proposition. **321**

To sell herbs, denote abundance. **722**

HERD—To dream of a herd of cattle, signifies that

you will realize your ambition. **712**

HERDSMAN—To see one, is a sign of intelligence. This dream denotes that you are very intellectual, and on account of your skill you are going to succeed well in life. **593**

HERO—Denotes a successful trip, filled with new joys and experience. **297**

HERRINGS—To eat them in your sleep signify low circumstances. **637**
To turn away from them, is a sign of good fortune on the following day. **369**

HICCUP—To dream of having an attack of hiccup, warns you to look after your stomach. It is advisable to consult a physician at once. Remember that health comes first. **226**

HICKORY NUTS—Denotes ill health and vexation. **261**

HIDE—To dream of hiding from any one, signifies that you will lose part of your savings through ignorance. **260**
To see others hide from you is a sign of power and wealth. **939**

HIGH BALL—To make a high ball, signifies a happy life filled with the sweet memories of the blessed past. This is an excellent dream to all, regardless of your present position. **777**

HIGH SCHOOL—To attend one, is a sign of long life and much happiness. It also promises a little wealth. **194**

HILL—To climb a hill denotes a successful career. **376**
If however you are unable to reach the top of the hill, it is a sign of failure at present. **735**

HINDU—To see one in your sleep denotes long life and sudden wealth. **736**
To talk to one, mark his words, that you may be benefited by them. **635**

HIP—To dream that your hip is swollen, denotes an
elaborate feast, and extensive drinking. **437**

HIRE—To dream of hiring any one signifies that you
will build up a tremendous business, on account
of your genius and learning. **270**
To dream that you are hired by some one, indicates
ordinary circumstances. **641**

HISTORY—To dream of reading or studying any kind
of history, denotes that you will visit historical
scenes. Some of these scenes will be of striking
solemnity. **333**

HIVE—Denotes small gain. **205**

HOE—Denotes you will receive a spiritual blessing.
327

HOISTING—To see anything hoist in the air, signifies
that you will rise far about your present stage
in life. It also signifies that your friends are faithful. **917**

HOLD UP—Denotes that a friend or relative will be
robbed. **256**

HOLE—To see a deep hole in the earth, signifies
that there will be death in the family shortly. **101**

HOLIDAY—To dream of a holiday, signifies that you
are now living a little above your means. This
dream warns you to check on your expenditure
in order that you may be able to save something
for times of adversity, and old age. **573**

HOME—To dream of being at home, signifies that
you will realize your hope shortly. This dream
also promises health and abundance of wealth. **763**

HOMELY PERSON—To see one in your sleep, denotes that you will attain success by your genius
and learning and not by your phisiology. **657**

HONEY—To dream of honey, denotes that your boy
friend is crazy about you. He is very jealous,
therefore you should be very careful in selecting

your company. To a man vice-versa. **294**

HONEYCOMB—To suck honey from a honeycomb, denotes love, that love no one knows. **276**

HOODOO—To dream of a hoodoo person, denotes that you will succeed in obtaining your wishes. You will discover a startling secret. **321**

HORIZON—To dream of the horizon, denotes a brilliant future. It is a sure sign of health, wealth and much happiness. **265**

HORN—To dream of a horn, signifies that the prisoner will be released at the final trial. **157**

HOROSCOPE—To dream of reading your own horoscope, denotes that you will go through life successfully. Your life will be of sunshine and laughter. **634**

To read the horoscope of others, denotes that you are surrounded by deceitful people, whom you call friends. **475**

HORRIBLE—To witness anything horrible, signifies disaster. **193**

HORSE—A grey horse signifies long life and happiness. **487**

A white horse, denotes that you will succeed in executing your plans. **573**

A sorrel horse is a sign of approaching marriage. **213**

A brown horse signifies that you will recover your losses. **467**

A dark horse, denotes that you will be married shortly. **272**

A dead horse, signifies danger and temptation. **529**

A chestnut horse signifies sudden wealth. **319**

HORSE GUARD—To see one in your sleep, denotes that you are well protected. Have no fear. You will succeed in executing your present plans. **428**

HORSE RACE—To witness one signifies great gain

and happiness. **310**

To dream of betting on a race signifies power. **341**

HORSE SHOE—To dream of one, denotes luck on the following. This is a very good dream to gamblers. **441**

HOSIERY—To dream of a beautiful pair of hosiery, denotes that your sweetheart is going to give you a very fine present. **786**

HOSPITAL—To visit one is a sign of worry and vexation. **216**

To visit a friend or relative in a hospital, denotes lost hopes. You will not succeed in executing your present plans. **635**

HOT—To dream of anything hot, signifies that you will be engaged in a heated argument. If precaution is not exercised this argument will likely develop into a fight. **021**

HOT HOUSE—To be confined in one denotes misery and loss of reputation. **011**

To see others in a hot house denotes business success. **519**

HOTEL—To visit one, signifies that you will rise far above your present position in life and be happy. **387**

HOTHEADED PERSON—To dream of a hotheaded person, signifies that you will cause a great deal of trouble, which will be un-intentional on your part. **111**

HOUSE—To see a house built of brick, signifies exceedingly good fortune. **237**

A wooden house denotes an unfortunate investment. **269**

An old house, denotes that you will receive a letter which will contain cheerful news. **441**

A new house, denotes that you will be happily married in the near future. **165**

HOUSE ON FIRE—To see a house on fire signifies grief. **300**
To dream of seeing a house saved from burning denotes long life and prosperity. **301**

HOUSEMAID—To see one denotes, that you will succeed in getting the job that you desire. **910**

HOUSETOP—Is a sign of elevation in life. **380**

HOUSEWORK—To dream of doing housework, denotes a peaceful and happy existence. It also denotes an increase in family. **597**

HUCKLEBERRIES—To dream of huckleberries, signify that you will have a thrilling vacation this season, filled with new experienies. **281**

HUMMING BIRD—To see one in your sleep, denotes that your disposition is very pleasant. On account of this, you will be instrumental in forming an organzation, which will be a great benefit to the community in which you are now living. From this great deed, you will be hailed as a benefator. **291**

HUMPBACK—To see a humpback person, denotes a scandal. **256**

HUNGRY—To dream of being hungry and unable to obtain food, denotes trouble and anxiety. **523** if you are able to get food in a short time it indicates success and much happiness. **711**

HUNTING—To dream of hunting, signifies that the sorrows of yesterday will be changed to the joys of today. This dream warns you to cheer up, and let by-gone be by-gone. Nothing but success is before you. **121**

HUNTER—To see one denotes courage and great ambition. It denotes a happy life. **329**

HURRICANE—To dream of one, denotes that your plans will be shattered. It is a sign of lost hope. **218**

HURRY—To dream of being in a hurry indicates that you will hear false news about your lover. **441**

HUSBAND—If a woman dreams of her husband it is a sign that she loves him dearly, and will do anything to make him happy. It also denotes, that the husband is sincere, but he is very jealous. There is really no true love without jealousy. **323**

HUT—To dream of a hut, signifies a pleasant trip. **277**

HYDRANT—To dream of a fire hydrant denotes that you will receive a letter which you had long hoped for. **941**

A water hydrant signifies prosperity. **946**

HYMN—To dream of singing a hymn, signifies that your life will be made of sunshine and sorrow. **193**

HYSTERICS—To see a person in hysterics, denotes that your enemies are more than a match for you. **675**

ICE—To dream of ice denotes cold friendship. **365**

To dream of a large block of ice, denotes scandal and treachery. **300**

To drink ice water is a sign of domestic tranquility. **716**

ICEBERG—To see one in your sleep, denotes that you will discover a startling secret. **675**

To dream that you are sailing in a ship and it strikes an iceberg, is a sign of lost hopes. If however you dream that you are unhurt, it denotes peace and satisfaction. **569**

ICE BOX—To see one in your sleep, denotes long life and much happiness. **490**

ICE CAP—Is a sign of illness. **376**

ICE CREAM—Denotes a prosperous marriage and many dutful cihildren. **198**

To dream that the ice cream melts denotes pregnancy to a woman. **931**

To a man loss of position. **516**

ICEMAN—To have one serve you with ice, denotes that you will become very prosperous, by thrift and economy. **261**

ICICLES—Denote a severe winter. **852**

IDENTIFY—To identify any one is a sign of good luck on the following day. It also promises some wealth. **418**

IDIOT—To see one in your sleep, denotes mistaken identity. **117**
To talk or quarrel with one, denotes that you will be the victim of slander and notoriety. **600**

IDLE—To see an idle person denotes profitable employment. It also indicates elevation. **352**

IDOLATRY—To dream of idolatry, denotes a wasted life. **611**

ILL—To dream that you are ill, signifies that you have no confidence in yourself. **382**

IMAGE—To dream of an image, signifies that you will have your photograph taken in a short time. **281**

IMITATE—To dream that you imitate any one, is a sign of worries, and misunderstanding among friends and relatives. **193**

IMMORAL—To dream of committing an immoral act, denotes that you will indulge in vile pleasure, such as extensive drinking and so forth. **235**

IMPLEMENTS OF WAR—To dream of such implements, is a sign of lost hopes. It also denotes vexation and impatience. **710**

IMPOSTER—To see one in your sleep, denotes that you will cause the down fall of one who is greatly opposed to you. **139**

INCENSE—To dream of burning sweet smelling incense, denotes that you will succeed in winning

the one that you love. You will be married shortly. **281**

INDIAN—To see one denotes that you will win a
sum of money. **311**

To quarrel with one, denotes power and dignity.
366

INDIAN CORN—Denotes a successful career. **369**

To gather it is a sign of happiness accompanied by
extraordinary good health. **875**

To plant it is a sign of domestic tranquility. **361**

INFANT—To see one in your sleep, denotes that you
ar a plain, simple, lovable person. You are therefore beloved by every one with whom you come
in contact. **211**

INFECTION—To dream of having any kind of infection, signifies that you will not receive any benefit
from the money that you have saved. **147**

INHALE—To dream of inhaling anything is a sign
of danger. **621**

INHERITANCE—To dream of an inheritance, denotes
joy and much profit. **193**

INJECTION—Denotes divorce proceedings or sepa-
ration. **281**

INJURY—To dream that you receive an injury, signifies that some one is trying to make you lose your
job. You should take care of your position. Do
your work well, and do not talk to any one during
working hours, unless it relates to your work. **591**

INJUSTICE—To dream that you are a victim of injustice, is a sign of discrimination. **126**

INK—Denotes that you will succeed in obtaining the
position you desire. **412**

To spill it is a sign disappointment. **216**

INKWELL—To see one in your sleep, denotes that
you will be honored, by prominent people. **384**

INQUIRY—To dream of an inquiry, denotes that you

are being slandered by your neighbors. They gossip about you every day. When they are talking to you they are laughing all the time. Do not help them laugh, for they are laughing at you. But you will out smart them before long. **516**

INSANE—To see one in your sleep, denotes that you will inherit a large fortune by the death of a friend or relative. **850**

INSANE ASYLUM—Denotes a profitable business enterprise. **833**

INSCRIPTION—To read one in your sleep denotes long life and prosperity. **692**

INSIDE LOOKING OUT—To dream of being inside looking out is a sign of sadness. **000**
To see others inside looking out denotes a gay life. **100**

INSPECTOR—To have one visit you, signifies that you will invest in a good paying proposition. Your income will be so great, that you will be able to retire in a short time, and live happily for the rest of your life. **341**

INSTALLMENT—To dream of buying anything on the installment plan, is a sign of peace and domestic happiness. **971**

INSTRUMENT—To dream of a musical instrument indicates that you will succeed socially as well as financially. **231**
To dream of playing one denotes kisses and caresses. **600**

INSULT—To be insulted denotes that it will be necessary to demand respect from a certain party in order to please your wife or husband. **224**

INSURANCE—To dream of one, denotes that your investment is secured. It also denotes sudden wealth accompanied by the picture of good health. **176**

To quarrel with an insurance collector, denotes that you will be independent in the near future. **309**

INTESTINE—To see any kind of intestine denotes sickness. **901**

INVALID—Denotes that you will form the acquaintance with one in power. This acquaintance will eventually develop into a marriage. **324**

INVENTOR—To dream of one, signifies an honorable and a very successful career. It also indicates that you are in the picture of good health. **239**
To dream that you yourself are an inventor, denotes that you will be placed in a good paying position, by one in power. **399**

INVEST—To invest in any enterprise, denotes that you will rise to an unlimited position, on account of your steadfastness of purpose. **252**

INVESTIGATOR—To see one denotes that you will overthrow your enemies in their foul undertakings. **876**

INVITATION—To dream of one, signifies that your wife or husband will return to you shortly, and never to leave home again, for love is too strong, both of you love each other dearly. **751**

IODOFORM—To dream of iodoform, denotes that you will be completely cured from the sickness from which you are now suffering. **173**

IRON—To dream of a piece of iron, denotes scandal and mischief. **736**

IRONING CLOTHES—To iron your own clothes, signifies that you will live to a ripe old age. Your life will be filled with great joy and happiness. It also indicates that you will at all times, maintain your daily wants, although you will never be rich. **327**

ISLAND—To dream of being on a small island, signifies a lonesome life. This dream warns you to cheer up, for skies are not always blue. **386**

ISRAELITE—To dream of an israelite is a sign of great joy and prosperity. This is a good dream to investors and other business people. **318**

ITALIAN—To see one in your sleep is a sign of a compromise in which you will be greatly benefited. **268**

ITCH—To dream of having the itch denotes sudden wealth. **826**

IVORY—Denotes loss in business. **389**

ITEMS—To dream of many items, signify that you will receive a sum of money from an unexpected source. **425**

JACKET—To dream of one denotes that you will form the acquaintance of a sophisticated person. **826**

To wear one is a sign of pleasure and courage. **261**

JACK KNIFE—To see one in your sleep, denotes a dangerous undertaking. **762**

To carry one, denotes impending danger. **365**

JAILER—To see one denotes that the prisoner will escape punishment by the skill of a witty lawyer. **576**

JAM—To eat it, signifies that your sweetheart is faithful. **393**

JAMAICAN—To dream of one, signifies that you will enter a profitable business. From this business you will realize a decent sum of money, and live happily. **284**

JANITOR—To dream that you are a janitor, signifies that you wil realize a little money in the near future. **217**

JAZZ—To attend a jazz party, denotes that you will meet your future wife or husband, within a few days, To a married man it denotes that he is jealous of his wife: to a woman vice-versa. **632**

JEALOUSY—To dream that you are jealous of anyone, denotes that you will exercise poor judgment
in transacting a certain business, which means a
great deal to you. Nevertheless, you will suceed
in this particular enterprise. 471

JELLYFISH—To eat a great deal of jellyfish, indicates that you will cause much trouble on account of the slip of your tongue. 221

JEWELER—To visit one, denotes that you will receive a costly present from your darling lover. 738

JEWELRY—To wear a great deal of expensive jewelry, denotes, that you are going to burst into society, and become very prominent in social affairs.
You will be the talk of the town. It also denotes
that you will take a trip to Monte Carlo in the
near future. 712

JEW'S HARP—To see a Jew's harp, signifies that
you will have a great many handsome children.
These children will make you very happy, for they
will be your sole support in your old age. 333

JOB—To dream that you have lost your job, signifies
that you are being slandered, by one of your so
called friends. Do not let any one know your business, for you are beng envied for your position.
181

JOCKEY—To see one, signifies that you will win a
great deal of money from some gambling enterprise. 219

JOINDER—To see one at work denotes wealth and
much happiness. 482
To speak to one denotes a speedy marriage. 646

JOY—To dream of enjoying one self denotes a peaceful mind and a happy ending of all of your troubles.
312

JOY RIDE—To go joy riding denotes a successful
career. You will be happily married in the near

future. To those who are already married, it promises sudden wealth. **347**

JOURNEY—To dream that you travel a far distance, signifies trouble and anxiety. **239**

JUDGE—To see one, denotes that you barely escape of being drawn into a plot, which would have brought about your downfall. **201**

JUMP—To dream that you jump from a high place, signifies that you will change your place of residence shortly. The change will be very advantageous to you. **764**

JUNGLE—To be in the jungle denotes a lonesome life. **234**

JUNK—To sell junk, denotes poverty, and vexation. **274**

JURY—To dream of the jury, denotes that you will be wrongly accused. But your innocence will be proved. **163**
To dream that you sit on the jury, signifies elevation of fortune. **732**

JUSTICE OF THE PEACE—To dream of the justice of the peace, denotes elopement. This is an excellent dream to lovers. **348**

KANGAROO—To see one in your sleep denotes that you will form the acquaintance of a selfish person. **942**

KEEL—To see the keel of a ship denotes that you will escape punishment. **566**

KEG—To see one in your sleep, denotes that you are being slandered maliciously. **377**

KEROSENE—Denotes sad news. To drink it denotes that you will suffer from a pain in your bowels. **319**

KETCHUP—To eat it signifies family quarrels. To turn away from it, denotes gratified ambition. **400**

KETTLE—A hot kettle denotes that you will receive

a visit from a friend, whom you have not seen, since school days. **316**

A cold kettle, denotes a chilly reception. **561**

KEYS—Denote security in one's affair. It also promises long life and happiness. **072**

KICK—To dream of being kicked, denotes that you have risen to the position, where you can demand respect. Your company should be well chosen. You cannot afford to associate with everyone. **137**

To dream that you kick any one, is a sign of power and dignity. **356**

KIDNAP—To dream that you are being kidnapped, signifies that some one is deeply in love with you. That person will do anything that you wish in order to marry you. **368**

KIDNEYS—To dream of your kidneys signify slander and temptation. **480**

Bad kidneys is a sign of danger. **764**

KILL—To dream that you kill anything is a sign of approaching danger. **423**

To dream that you are being killed, denotes long life and much happiness. **349**

KIMONO—Denotes excessive love affairs. It is really a sign of enjoyable pleasure. **144**

KINDNESS—To receive an act of kindness from any one in your sleep is a sign of anxiety in business. **531**

KING—To see a king sitting upon a throne, denotes that you will become very prominent in social circles. **432**

To quarrel with a king is a sign of cheating. **314**

KINKY HAIR—To see a person with this kind of hair denotes ambition and prosperity. **606**

KISS—To kiss a pretty maid, denotes that some one is madly in love with you. **347**

To kiss an old maid, denotes secret sorrows. **456**

To kiss your parents denote that you will obtain their forgiveness. **397**

To kss the earth, denotes humiliation. **344**

KIT—To dream of carrying a lunch kit, signifies that you will be a working man or woman all the days of your life. **193**

KITCHEN—To dream of being in your own kitchen, denotes peace and satisfaction. It also indicates a reunion among old friends and relatives. **369**

KITE—This is an excellent dream. It promises wealth and much happiness. **091**

KITTENS—To see many kittens, denote that you will have a baby boy, who will become a physician and surgeon. **728**

KNEEL DOWN—To dream that you kneel down, is a warning of reform. You should attend your church more regular. **181**

KNITTING—To dream of knitting, signifies that you are a lovely person, very sympathetic and loving. You are just a darling. You are being loved and respected by all for your fine qualities and charming disposition. **433**

KNOCKOUT—To witness one denotes great speculation and other profitable investments. **562**

To dream that some one knocks you out signifies failure **556**

KNOWLEDGE—To dream that you possess a great deal of knowledge denotes a pleasant and profitable trip. **752**

KU-KLUX-KLAN—To dream of this order of men, signifies that you will overthrow a dangerous enemy. **000**

LABELS—To dream of labels signify prosperity. **867**

LABORATORY—To see one in your sleep, denotes hard work but good pay. **374**

To work in one, signifies that you will **succeed**

in putting across a certain proposition. **542**

LABOR DAY—To dream of this day, is a sign of joy and much happiness. **183**

LABOR UNION—To join one, signifies that you will rise to an honorable position. **144**

LACE—To see a great deal of lace, denotes that you will meet a person who will propose marriage to you. **176**

LAME—To see a lame person, denotes a dangerous ous enemy. You should read the seventy-first psalm for nine consecutive days. It reads thus: "In thee, O Lord, do I put my trust; let me never be put to confusion, etc. **566**

LADDER—To climb a ladder, signifies much prosperity. **394**

To descend one, is a sign of failure. **367**

LADY—To see a pretty lady denotes joy and profit. **316**

A naked shapely lady denotes extremely good fortune on the following day. **372**

If the lady, happens to be ugly, it denotes that you will be placed in a trying position. **563**

If you laugh at the lady, it signifies that you will be dishonored. **388**

To dream that you are being kissed by a shapely lady, denotes an honorable career. **569**

To see a pregnant lady, denotes profitable investments. **116**

LAKE—A lake of pure, clear water denotes success. **317**

A lake of muddy water is a sign of losses. **585**

LAMP—To see a lamp burning bright, signifies that you will rise to great power, through your education. **500**

A dim burning lamp, signifies slow progress. **361**

LAMP POST—To see one in your sleep, denotes that

you will receive a fairly good return on the money you have invested. **399**

LAND—To dream of owning a great deal of land, denotes a successful career. **409**

LANDLADY—To argue with her, denotes that your enemies are more than a match for you. **670**
To quarrel, and then make up, signifies gratified ambition. **061**

LANDLORD—To see one in your sleep, denotes that you will succeed in raising the money that you desire. **332**

LANDSCAPE—To see one in your sleep, denotes that you will visit a historical scene of intense solemnity. **398**

LANGUAGE—To dream that you are learning or speaking foreign language, denotes that you will take a pleasant trip across the open country, and the fertile meadows. **291**

LANTERN—To carry one, denotes that you will go through life undaunted; you will face life with reality. **185**

LARD—To dream of lard, signifies that you will marry a kind hearted person of strong integrity. **431**

LARK—To hear one sing, signifies that you will succeed in obtaining your wish. It also denotes that you will discover the truth about a certain affair, for which you had long desired. **273**

LAUGH—To dream that you laugh, signifies a peaceful mind. **234**

LAUNDRY—To work in one, denotes that you will meet a hard working person, who will propose marriage to you. Should you accept this offer, you will be happily married in a few months. **781**

LAUNDRESS—To dream of one, denotes embarrassment. **519**

LAW—To dream of the law denotes that some one

will deceive you. **561**

To dream of breaking the law denotes weakness of mind. **356**

To uphold the law is a sign of thrift and happiness. **362**

LAW SUIT—Denotes a quarrel with one in power. **637**

LAWN—To play upon a lawn, signifies that you will rise to a high position by your own genius and learning. **184**

LAWYER—To see one, denotes business success. **384**

To quarrel with one, denotes lost hopes. **329**

LAXATIVE—Is a sign of domestic quarrels and dissatisfaction. **328**

LAZY PERSON—To see one denotes that you are scolded for mingling into the affairs of others. **725**

LEAD—To dream of lead, signifies a great deal of worry. You should stop worrying, because everything is going to clear up suddenly. **033**

LEAD PENCIL—To use one in your sleep, denotes that you will win a sum of money shortly. **123**

LEAK—To dream that your house leaks, signifies a sad life. **549**

LEAP—To leap from a high place denotes loss of position and prestige. **220**

LEAP YEAR—Denotes that you will meet with a great deal of success next year. It also signifies an increase in family by the birth of a child. **321**

LEATHER—To see a great deal of leather denotes a contented life. **537**

To wear leather clothes signifies an adventurous undertaking. **156**

LEAVES—To dream of green leaves is a sign of approaching death to some one dear to you. **368**

Yellow leaves denote a prosperous adventure. **278**

To gather dry leaves denote domestic happiness. **201**

LEASE—To sign one denotes that you will succeed in holding your present job for a long time. It further denotes that you are becoming efficient in your task. **536**

LECTURE—To dream that you lecture, signifies that your mind is now at ease. Your troubles are over, you can now look forward to prosperity. **623**

LEGS—To dream of pretty legs denote joy and happiness. **291**
Skinny legs is a sign of sickness. **129**

LEGGINGS—To wear them, denote that you will be called upon to fill an important position in your community. **153**

LEG-OF-MUTTON—To dream of having a leg of mutton, signifies, that you will be very prosperous next year. **235**

LEMON—To eat, one signifies that you are surrounded by powerful enemies who wish to ruin your good name. Read the thirty-eight psalm: "Unto thee will I cry, O Lord my rock"; etc. **538**

LEMONADE—To drink it signifies health, wealth and much happiness. **041**

LEOPARD—To dream of a leopard, denotes that your wife or husband loves you a great deal. To a man his wife is very faithful, to a woman vica-versa. **417**

LEPER—To dream that you have this disease, denotes a great deal of sickness. This sickness will be attributed to your own carelessness and negligence. **740**

LETTER—To dream of writing a letter, signifies that you will succeed in marrying the person that you love. This marriage will be one of great success. **769**

LETTER CARRIER—To see one in your sleep, denotes that you will receive a letter which will contain good news. **256**

LETTUCE—To eat, it denotes wealth and long life. **512**

To turn away from it, denotes a dreary life. **367**

LIAR—To dream that you are branded as a liar, is a sign of wealth and prominence. **065**

To call anyone a liar in your sleep denotes that you will commit an act of injustice, which will be unintentional on your part. **634**

LIBRARY—To visit one, denotes great learning and popularity among the opposite sex. **205**

To see others reading in a library denotes that some one is trying to undermine you. **275**

LICE—To dream of a grtat deal of lice, is a sign of sudden wealth obtained through games of chances. You will be lucky for a long time. **748**

LICENSE—To dream of obtaining any kind of a license, denotes great success on the following day. **281**

LICENSE BUREAU—Denotes great success in industry and commerce. **766**

LIE—To dream of telling a lie, signifies that you will cause a great deal of trouble to your friend or family by talking a little too much. **338**

LIEUTENANT—Denotes joy and much profit. **633**

To quarrel with one, denotes that you will be cheated out of your rights. **635**

LIFEBOAT—To see one in your sleep, denotes that you will render a charitable act to one who is greatly in need. **288**

LIFE GUARD—To see one denotes a comfortable life. It also denotes that your partner is sincere. **436**

LIGHT— To dream of a bright light, denotes great success. **450**

A dim light is a sign of failure. **376**

LIGHTHOUSE—To see one in your sleep, denotes that you will travel shortly. It also denotes that you will be comfortably rich. **316**

LIGHTNING—To dream of lightning, signifies that someone is tryng to break up the happiness of your home by making love to your wife or husband. **283**

LILAC FLOWERS—Denotes love and romance. **662**

LILY—To dream of a pretty lily, signifies that you will receive a declaration of love from your sweetheart. **223**

LIMES—To dream of limes denote wealth by dishonest means. **516**

LIMOUSINE—Denotes joy and much profit. **281**
To ride in one, signifies that some one, whom you do not know at present is crazy about you. **300**

LINEN—To see a great deal of linen, denotes that you are going to enter a good paying business shortly. **173**
Unclean linens is a sign of failure. **517**

LINIMENT—To use it, signifies a dirty disease. **735**

LINOLEUM—To dream that you have a new piece of linoleum, denotes that you will own a beautiful home in the near future. **251**

LINSEED OIL—Denotes disgrace. **518**

LION—To fight with one, and overthrow him, denotes that you will foul your enemies. **737**
If the lion overpowers you, it denotes that your enemies are more than a match for you. **566**
To play with a lion, signifies that you are a person of indomitable courage, and as a result you are obliged to succeed in your undertaking. **525**

LIPS—To dream of having well formed lips denotes that you will meet some one whom you have not seen for many years. **007**

To dream of having long lips is a sign of gossip. **867**

Beautiful formed lips signify long life and prosperity. **701**

LIQUOR—To dream of partaking of a great deal of liquor, signifies joy and profit. **219**

LITERATURE—To dream of reading English Literature denotes that you will come in contact with a person of culture and literary ability. **565**

LIVER—To dream of a fatty liver denotes that you drink too much liquor. **532**

To dream of calf's or any other kind of liver signifies that your friends are faithful and they will come to your assistance. both financially and otherwise. **252**

LIZARD—To see one in your sleep, denotes that you will accumulate wealth slowly but surely. **236**

LOAD—To dream of carrying a heavy load, denotes that you will lose a part of your savings in a wild cat scheme. **563**

LOAD STONE—To see one in your sleep indicates that some one is trying to rob you out of your savings. **539**

To sell lodestone denotes a successful business transaction. **911**

LOAN—To dream of borrowing money from any one, denotes lost friendship. **309**

LOBSTERS—To eat them denote a successful career. **235**

To turn from them, denote secret sorrows. **540**

LOCK—To see one in your sleep, denotes security in business. **630**

LOCKER—Denotes great learning. **758**

LOCKSMITH—Denotes security in business. **372**

LOCOMOTIVE—To see one in your sleep, denotes a brilliant future. **733**

To drive one, denotes sudden wealth. **485**

LODESTONE—Denotes joy and happiness. It also denotes that the one whom you love will return shortly. **745**

LODGING HOUSE—To live in one, signifies that you will save a great deal of money from your present earnings. **316**

LOGS—To see them in your sleep denotes security in all kinds of business trade or profession. **518**

LOLLIPOPS—To eat them denotes that you will regain your health. **371**

To load them on a wagon signifies hard work but good pay. **681**

LONGSHOREMAN—To dream of one, signifies that you will be caught stealing from your employer. Nevertheless, you will not be punished. **576**

LOOKING GLASS—To see yourself in a glass, denotes that you have a great many admirers. **451**

LOOPHOLE—To look through a loophole, signifies shame and embarrassment. **492**

LOSE—To dream of losing anything denotes small profits. **932**

If a woman dreams of losing her engagement or wedding ring, it denotes that her husband is in love with some one else. **728**

LOTTERY—Denotes good luck in games of chances on the following day. **736**

LOVE-SICK—To dream of being love-sick is a sign of jealousy and weakness on your part. **518**

LUCKY—To dream that you are lucky indicates good fortune in games of chances and other business enterprise. **644**

LUGGAGE—To dream of a luggage, signifies that you will suffer loss which will be attributed to your own carelessness. **459**

LUMBER—To dream of lumber signifies new hopes,

new friends, and a new life. **434**

LUNATIC—Denotes mad and passionate love affairs. **976**

LUNCH—To dream of taking lunch denotes peace and satisfaction. **932**

To take others to lunch is a sign of infatuation for one whom you are in contact with daily. **933**

LUXURY—To dream of any kind of luxury, denotes wealth and much happiness. **735**

LYE—To dream of lye is a sign of regrets. **163**

MACARONI—To eat it in your sleep, denotes that you will rise to an unlimited position in life. You will therefore acquire wealth easily. **539**

MACHINE—To dream of one, signifies a misunderstanding among friends and relatives. **187**

To operate one, is a sign of wealth and happiness. **500**

MACKEREL—is a sign of profitable employment. **296**

MAD—To see a madman or mad woman denotes that you contemplate in your far seeing contemplations, and baffle things in your own design. **508**

To dream of being mad is a sign of sadness. **085**

MADAM—To dream of a heavy set madam, signifies a great deal of pleasure. **152**

MADHOUSE—To read one, denotes that you will receive a letter from one in need. **177**

MAGIC—Denotes an increase of knowledge and greater contact with prominent people. **834**

MAGICIAN—To see one in your sleep, denotes that you will discover a secret which will benefit you financially. **429**

To quarrel with one, denotes that you are being slandered by your relatives. **566**

MAGISTRATE—To see one in your sleep, denotes that you will escape trouble by using keen judgment. **102**

MAGNET—To dream of a magnet, denotes that your sweetheart is true to you. His love is as strong as death. **276**

MAGNIFYING GLASS—To see one in your sleep, denotes that you will become wealthy as the years roll on. **561**

MAHOGANY—To have a mahogany bedstead denotes that you will receive a declaration of love from your sweetheart. **776**

MAID—To dream of having a maid, denotes power and dignity. **345**

To quarrel with one, denotes that you are being envied. **599**

MAIL—To dream of mailing a letter signifies profitable investments. **361**

To dream of working in a mail department is a sign of benevolence. **936**

To dream that you are a mail carrier denotes prosperity and good health. **594**

MAN—To dream of a tidy colored man, denotes good fortune in games of chances. **752**

A white man denotes money by dishonest means. **543**

A man dressed in white, denotes an honorable career. **789**

A strange man, denotes grief and vexation. **540**

Man in bed denotes an abundance of pleasure. **490**

A man dressed in black denotes secret sorrows. **566**

An old man, denotes that you will be the victim of slander. **444**

A one-eyed man, denotes that you generally form wrong opinions about the affairs of others. **219**

MANAGER—To dream of a manager, denotes that you will invest in a well paying proposition. You will therefore accumulate a large sum of money. **508**

MANDACOO—Denotes a pleasant voyage across the country, or to some distant land. 635

MANDOLIN—To play one, denotes wealth and happiness. 297
To hear one play is a sign of good fortune on the following day. 281

MANGOES—To see ripe mangoes in your sleep signify an abundance of wealth. 165
Green mangoes is a sign of disappointment. 481
To sell them denote much happiness and the termination of all your troubles. 659
To gather them indicate a loving wife or husband. 936

MANICURE—To dream of having your finger nails manicured, signify, that you will lead a sporty life in the near future. 435

MANSLAUGHTER—To dream of manslaughter, denotes a tiresome and dreary life. 589

MANTLE—Denotes that you will go shopping with one of your friends next week. This friend is very sincere. 295

MANUFACTURE—To dream that you are in the manufacturing business, denotes prosperity and health. 491

MAP—To dream of a map, denotes extensive travel. 281

MARATHON DANCE—Denotes that you are leading a gay life. 248

MARBLES—To pitch marbles denote that you will rise by the downfall of one in power. 111

MARBLESTONE—To dream of a marble stone, denotes the death of a relative or near friend. 511

MARKET—To visit one, denotes that you will receive an expensive gift from your sweetheart. 071

MARRY—To dream that you are about to be married, denotes the death of a relative or friend. 288

MARSHAL—To dream of a marshal, denotes that you will receive a dispossess from your landlord. **567**

MASK—To wear one, denotes that you will try to hide a secret, which will be known by and by. **193**

MASQUERADE—To see one in your sleep, denotes that you will meet a lovely person at a party. That person will become your sweetheart. In a few months you will hear the wedding bells. **728**

MASSACRE—To dream of a massacre, denotes lost hopes and ambition. **193**

MASSAGE—To dream of having a massage, denotes that your blood is out of order. This dream warns you to take a blood tonic. **676**

MASS MEETING—To attend one, denotes that you will invest in a well paying enterprise. **161**

MAT—To see one denotes that you will be ill treated and discriminated by one in power. **944**

MATCH—To dream of a match, signifies that one of your friends will meet with a slight accident. **293**

MATHEMATICS—To dream of mathematics, denotes that your number will show up in a few days. **267**

MATTRESS—To dream of a mattress, signifies that your wife or husband is unfaithful. **287**

MAYOR—To dream of the mayor denotes that you secure a governmental position in the near future. **117**

MEADOW—To cross a meadow, denotes that you will receive a great deal of love from your darling sweetheart. **674**

MEASURE—To measure anything, denotes that you will be victorious in a court of justice. **936**

MECHANIC—To dream of one signifies, that you

will succeed in executing your plans. **379**

MEDAL—To be the recipient of a medal, denotes that you will be greatly honored for your ambition and respectability. **498**

MEDICINE—To dream of taking medicine, signifies that you will visit a friend who is a little indisposed. **297**

MELON—To eat melon, signifies that you will suffer from a headache. **144**

MEMORY—To dream of heaving a good memory signifies that you will learn the truth about that, which was supposed to be a mystery. **418**

To dream of having poor memory denotes grief. **368**

MENDING—To mend or make your clothes, portrays that you will exercise good judgment in solving your present affairs. You should therefore proceed to execute your plans immediately. **637**

To see others mending, is a sign of profitable employment. **783**

MRCHANT—To dream of one, denotes great prosperity. **416**

MERCY—To dream of begging for mercy, denotes that you are a coward. **295**

MERMAID—To dream of one denotes a fantastic life. **475**

If they hide from it denotes secret sorrow. **100**

MERRY MAKING—To dream of making merry, denotes that you will win the one that you love. **964**

To see others enjoying themselves, is a sign of great consideration for your oponent. **797**

MESSAGE—To receive one indicates much happiness and prosperity. **158**

To send a message is a sign of distress. **225**

MESSENGER—To see one in your sleep, denotes health and prosperity. **119**

METAL—Signifies profitable investment. **945**

METER—To dream of any kind of a meter, denotes that you will be successful in a court of justice. **275**

MICE—To dream of mice denote the downfall of your enemies. **149**

MICROSCOPE—To see one denotes that you will succeed in obtaining your objective. **445**

To see others looking through a microscope, signifies that you will discover a startling truth about something that will interest you a great deal. **644**

MIDDY BLOUSE—To dream of one denotes that you are admired a great deal for the manner in which you conduct yourself. **366**

To see others wearing a middy blouse signifies that you will obtain your goal in a very short time. **010**

MIDWIFE—To see one, signifies family quarrels. **527**

If a woman sees a midwife wearing a uniform, it denotes that she will have a son, who will become a doctor. **769**

MILESTONE—To see one in your sleep, denotes a journey on foot. **441**

MILK—To drink milk, denotes that you will receive a declaration of love from your sweetheart. To turn away from it signifies unrequieted love. **441**

MILKMAID—To see one in your sleep denotes that you will marry a good looking and reliable person. **563**

MILKMAN—To see one in your sleep, denotes great prosperity and much happiness. It also indicates extraordinary health. **561**

To argue with him, is a sign that you will be cheated out of a little money. **500**

MILL—To see a mill in operation, denotes a very brilliant future. **329**

If the mill is at stand still, it denotes slow, but sure

progress. **537**

MILLIONAIRE—To dream of one, denotes that you
will marry a rich rascal. **101**

To a man, he will marry a virtuous young girl. **569**

MILLWRIGHT—Denotes hard work, but good pay.
139

To see one, making a mill, denotes a prosperous and
happy life. **129**

MIND READER—To see one, denotes that you will
go through life successfully. **246**

To quarrel with one, denotes that you will not succeed in obtaining the position that you desire. **356**

MINE—To work in a gold mine, denotes a brilliant
future. **356**

A silver mine, denotes ordinary circumstances. **516**

A coal or salt mine, denotes poverty. **064**

MINER—To see one in your sleep, denotes that you
will form the acquaintance of prominent people,
who will aid you financially. **539**

MINERAL—To dream of any kind of mineral, denotes that you will have a very pleasant vacation.
114

MINISTER—To dream of a minister, denotes that you
will regain the good will of your parents, which
means a great deal to you. **527**

To quarrel with one, signifies lost hope. **119**

MIRROR—To see one, denotes that you will win a
large sum of money shortly. **129**

MISCONDUCT—To dream of misconducting yourself
before any one is a sign of ill health. **101**

MISER—To see one in your sleep denotes vexation.
383

MISFORTUNE—To dream of having misfortune is
a sign of riches and much happiness. **426**

MOAN—To dream that you moan, signifies a pleasant
surprise. **519**

MOB—To see a crowd of people, denotes that there will arise a problem in your community which will cause a great deal of discussion. **279**

MOCK—To make fun at any one, denotes that you are being slandered by your neighbors. **271**

MODEL—To dream of a pretty model, denotes that you will fall in love with your employer. **387**

MOHAMMEDAN—To see one in your sleep denotes that you will have many wives or husbands. **483**
To quarrel with one is a sign of grief. **346**

MOLASSES—To dream of molasses, denotes long life and good fortune. **381**
To drink it, denotes that your wife or husband is faithful. **397**

MONASTERY—To visit one, denotes a dreary and wasted life. **911**
To leave one, denotes a successful career. **156**

MONGOOSE—Denotes riches and honor. **418**

MONEY—To see a great deal of money denotes that you will enter a good paying proposition. **576**
To count it, denotes power and dignity. **593**
To change money, denotes good fortune. **299**
To give away money, denotes power and dignity. **588**
To dream of silver money, is a sign of disappointment. **232**
Gold money denotes that you will win a large sum of money in a few days, and from this money, you will acquire additional wealth. **533**
Counterfeit money, denotes that you are underpaid for your labor. **535**
Paper money, denotes sudden wealth. It also indicates a brilliant future. **765**

MONITOR—To dream that you are a monitor, denotes that you will hold an important position in the near future. **243**

MONKEY—To see one, in your sleep. denotes that you will transact a great deal of business, with a very smart person. Be careful in drawing up and signing contracts, etc. **415**

MONSTER—To dream of a hairy monster, denotes excessive pleasure. It also denotes a great deal of drinking. **189**

MONUMENT—To visit one, denotes that you will see something of great curiosity. **714**

MOON—To dream of full moon denotes success in love and courtship. **516**
A young moon denotes that you will succeed in obtaining your wishes after a struggle. **518**

MOONLIGHT—To dream of the moonlight, denotes a brilliant future is in store for you. Ths is an excellent dream to all, especially lovers. It is truly a dream which clearly indicates success. **233**

MOP—To use one, denotes ordinary circumstances. **317**

MORGUE—To visit one, denotes death in the family. **546**

MORRIS CHAIR—To dream of a Morris chair, denotes that you will receive a pension for life. You will therefore live comfortable for the balance of your days, surrounded by loved ones. **219**

MORTAR—To see a great deal of mortar, denotes that you will own a beautiful home in the near future. **743**

MORTGAGE—To dream of a mortgage, denotes that you will invest your money wisely. **123**

MOSQUITOES—To dream of mosquitoes, denote that you are surrounded by powerful enemies. **591**

MOTHER—To see her in your sleep, denotes that she is in need of your help. If she is dead, it is a warning of reform. If she speaks to you follow her instructions carefully. **271**

MOTHER-IN-LAW—To dream of your mother-in-law, is a sign of quarrels and discontent. **286**

MOTOR BOAT—Denotes a great deal of pleasure and amusements among friends and relatives. **569**

MOTOR BUS—To drive in one, denotes that you are going on a picnic shortly. **261**

MOTOR CYCLE—To ride on one, denotes that you will rise to an honorable position by and by. **394**

MOTORMAN—To dream of a motorman, denotes that you will succeed in buying an automobile. **506**
To talk to one, denotes that you will pass a certain examination. **529**

MOUNTAIN—To climb a high mountain, denotes a brilliant future. **369**
If you are unable to reach the peak of the mountain, it denotes slow progress or probably failure. **541**

MOURN—To dream that you mourn signfies that one of your friends will cause you a great deal of trouble unintentionally. **213**

MOUTH ORGAN—To hear one play, denotes joy and profit. **256**
To play one yourself is a sign of approaching marriage. **260**

MOUSTACHE—To dream of having a beautiful moustache denotes wisdom. **125**
To see others with a long moustache denotes prestige. **620**

MOVE—To dream that you change your present abode, denotes an elevation in fortune. **965**

MOVING PICTURE—To see one denotes that you will now enjoy the blessing of peace and prosperity which you had so long desired. **194**

MUD—To dream of mud denotes slander and treachery. **121**

MULE—To ride on the back of a mule, denotes hard work, but nevertheless you will be well paid. **202**

To see a great deal of mules, indicate that you will overcome your enemies. **276**

MULTIPLY—To dream that you do a multiplication example, denotes that you will be very prosperous about the ending of this year. **314**

MUFFINS—To dream of muffins, denote very good luck to policy players. **193**

MUMPS—Denote a legacy by a relative. **139**

MURDER—To witness one, signifies trouble and anxiety. **533**

MURDERER—To see one in your sleep denotes loss

MUSEUM—To visit one, denotes that you will become famous in the near future. **564**

MUSHMELLONS—Denote good news. **431**

To give them away denote health and happiness. **511**

To eat them, denote that you will meet an old friend whom you have not seen, since school days. **543**

MUSHROOMS—To dream of mushrooms, denote a bad plague. **571**

MUSIC—To hear sweet music, denotes much happiness. **286**

Poorly played music denotes sickness. **088**

To hear discordant music signify loss of health. **912**

MUSLIN—To dream of muslin denotes that you will be envied by your neighbors for your nice clothes and neat appearance. **615**

To purchase a piece of muslin signifies that you will realize your life's ambition. **910**

MUSTARD—To dream of mustard, denotes that you will become wealthy by and by. **540**

MUSTARD PLASTER—Denotes that you will visit a sick friend. **544**

MUTTON—To dream of mutton signifies that your lover is true to you. **631**

To eat it denotes wealth. **225**

MYRTLE—To dream of this tree denotes that you will succeed in raising a lovely family of boys and girls. This is truly an excellent dream to a newly married couple. **112**

MYSTERY—To dream that you are able to solve a mystery, denotes that you will discover a startling secret. **761**

NAILS—To dream of nails, denote ordinary circumstances. **183**

To see a carpenter nailing, denotes that you will catch the one who is robbing you. **235**

NAKED—To see a naked person, denotes misery. **688**

If the person is shapely, it signifies, that you will marry the person to whom you are now engaged. **687**

To dream that you are naked, signifies lost hopes. **777**

NAMES—To dream that you have many names, denotes that you will get money, by dishonest means. **359**

To dream that people call you names, is a sign of contention. **355**

NAPKINS—Clean napkins, denote that you will succeed in executing your plans. **147**

NARCOTIC—To dream of any kind of narcotic, denotes that you are wasting your time on some one who is undesirable. **716**

NAUGHTY—To dream of a naughty child, signifies that your wife or husband is going to give you a severe scolding. **537**

NAVEL—To dream of an abnormal navel, denotes a weak mind. **371**

NAVY—Denotes long life and much happiness. It indicates extremely good health. **718**

To dream that you enlist in the navy, denotes protection of your affairs. 753

NECKLACE—To purchase a necklace, denotes that some one is deeply in love wih you. 372

To wear one around your neck, denotes joy and happiness. 529

To see others wearing a beautiful necklace denotes that you will succeed in getting the position you wish. 534

NEEDLES—To dream of needles, denote that you will get a laborious job, but nevertheless, you will receive big wages. 135

NEGRO—To see one in your sleep denotes an honorable and successful career. 121

To quarrel with one, denotes disaster. 321

NEIGHBOR—To dream of your neighbor, denotes that some one is trying to mingle into your business. Do not let your left hand know what your right hand is doing. 312

NEPHEW—To see your nephew in your sleep, denotes that you will invest in a gambling proposition. 276

NERVOUS—To see a nervous person in your sleep, denotes that you will cause a great deal of trouble to one who is in opposition to you. 519

NERVES—To dream of bad nerves is a sign of distress. 381

NEST—To see one in your sleep denotes joy and profit. 228

To see birds in their nest denotes a loving wife or husband. It also denotes success in business. 648

NET—To see a hair net, denotes that you are in the picture of good health. 272

A fisherman's net, denotes profit and loss. 500

NEURALGIA—To suffer from neuralgia denotes good luck in games of chances on the following day 765

To the unemployed it promises steady position. **369**

NEWS—To dream of receiving good news indicates a pleasant journey. **415**

Bad news indicate the loss of appetite. **516**

NEWSBOY—To see one in your sleep, denotes that you will hear of a murder in which you will be interested. **147**

To dream that you yourself are a newsboy, denotes a profitable investment. **400**

NEWSPAPER—To dream of a newspaper, denotes that you will receive a letter, which will contain good news. **131**

NEWSSTAND—To see one in your sleep, denotes a pleasant surprise. It also portrays that your business will improve as the years go by. **327**

To make a purchase from a newsstand, is a sign of intelligence and prosperity. **275**

NEW TESTAMENT—To dream of the new testament, denotes that you are religiously inclined. **111**

NEW YEAR—To dream of the New Year, signifies that your hopes and visions will be realized in a very short time. You will therefore have much, in which to be thankful for having obtained. **645**

NEW YORK—To dream of this city is a sign of prosperity and much happiness. **870**

NIECE—Denotes security in business and love affairs. **932**

To quarrel with your niece denotes disappointment. **424**

NIGHT—To dream of night, denotes that you are about to lose part of your savings. **873**

NIGHT GOWN—To wear one denotes pleasure. **641**

A silk night gown denotes long life, pleasure and good fortune. **369**

A cotton night gown is a sign of wealth. **426**

NIGHT MARE—To dream of one denotes a disturbed

mind. **085**

NIGHT WALK—To dream of taking a night walk
　　denotes sudden wealth and popularity. **871**

NOISE—To dream of hearing a great deal of noise
　　in your sleep, denotes a sorrowful life. **516**

NORTH POLE—To dream of the North Pole denotes
　　that you will receive a chilly reception from one
　　of your so called friends. **516**

　　To dream of reaching the North Pole denotes you
　　will receive a sum of money shortly from an un-
　　expected source. **036**

NORTHERNER—To dream of one denotes wealth,
　　and much happiness. **348**

NOSE—Denotes sudden joy and prosperity. **715**

NOTARY—To see one in your sleep, denotes that
　　you will be very successful in business. **745**

　　To quarrel with one denotes that you will lose part
　　of your savings. **764**

NOTEBOOK—To dream of a note book, denotes great
　　learning. **429**

NUDE—To see a nude person, denotes pleasure fol-
　　lowed by shame. **051**

NUMBERS—To dream of numbers denote wealth
　　and much happiness. There are peculiarities about
　　numbers: a six is a nine and vice-versa; three is
　　a five or a eight. A four is relative to zero. **609**

NUN—To see one in your sleep, denotes homage. **163**

NURSE—Denotes pregnancy. **572**

　　To quarrel wth a nurse, denotes that you will barely
　　escape of being drawn into a plot. **513**

　　To kiss a pretty nurse, denotes a profit by a serious
　　undertaking. **618**

NURSERY—Denotes ill health. **705**

NUTS—To dream of nuts, denote sad news. **111**

　　To eat them denotes slander. **581**

　　To turn away from them denotes prosperity. **569**

NUT CRACKER—To dream of a nut cracker, denotes a pleasant journey, which will be very advantageous to you in later years. **198**

NUTMEG—To grater nutmeg, denotes a happy reunion of friends and relatives. **323**

OAKTREE—Denotes profitable employment. It also indicates the emblem of peace and prosperity, followed by years of fruitfulness. **386**

OAR—To see one in your sleep, denotes a trip across water. **717**

OATH—To take an oath, denotes dishonesty. **320**

OATMEAL—To drink oatmeal, signifies jealousy on the part of your neighbors. **592**
To turn away from it, signifies that you will aid a poor person financially. **333**

OCEAN—To dream of the ocean, signifies that a great deal of trouble will befall one of your friends. **154**

OBSCENE LANGUAGE—To dream of using obscene language, denotes losses. **111**

OCTAGON FIGURE—Denotes that you are being slandered by one of your so called friends. **297**

OFFENSE—To dream that you commit an act of offense, signifies want. **665**

OFFICER—To see an officer of the law, denotes protection. It also denotes good luck on the following day. **367**

OFFICE BOY—To see one in your sleep, denotes that you will invest in stocks and bonds in the near future. **671**

OIL—To see an abundance of oil in your sleep signifies happiness and wealth. **761**
To spill oil denotes sickness. **815**

OILCLOTH—To dream of a piece of oilcloth, denotes that you will own a beautiful home in the near future. **413**

OILSTONE—To dream of an oilstone, indicates that you will have a son, who will become a master mechanic. **494**

OIL WELL—To dream of seeing oil spouting from a well, denotes riches in proportion to the amount of oil. **283**

OINTMENT—To dream of any kind of ointment, denotes that you will suffer from a slight pain in the chest or stomach. **771**

OLD LADY—To see an old lady denotes reform. If she talks to you, mark her words, so that you may be benefited by them. **257**

To quarrel with her denotes shame. **627**

OLD—To dream of one denotes gain. **256**

OLD MAID—To see one in your sleep, denotes that you are being robbed out of your labor. **176**

OLD TESTAMENT—To read the Old Testament denotes that you are living an honorable life. **152**

OLIVES—To dream of olives denotes that you are religiously inclined. **614**

ONIONS—To dream of onions in your sleep, denote that you will suffer want which will be the direct result of your own negligence and inertness. **962**

OPEN AIR—To dream of being in the open air, denotes that a brilliant future is in store for you. **059**

OPERA—To dream of an opera, signifies gratified ambition. **291**

OPERA SINGER—To hear one sing, is a sign of content. It also denotes that you will succeed in executing your plans. **665**

OPERATION—To dream of undergoing an operation is a sign of misery. **415**

To dream of others undergoing an operation, denotes that you will be wrongly accused. **534**

OPIUM—To dream of opium denotes that you will

attend an important trial in the near future. **203**

ORANGES—To dream of oranges, denote great success. It also denotes good health. **625**

ORATOR—To hear one lecture, denotes a happy and prosperous life. **509**
To oppose an orator, is a sign of strife and contention. **549**

ORCHARD—To walk through an orchard, denotes great happiness accompanied by great wealth. **218**
To see others, walking through an orchard, denotes love affairs. **497**

ORGAN—To hear one play denotes joy and much happiness. **197**
To play one yourself denotes that you will succeed in holding the one that you love. **548**

ORGANIST—To see one in your sleep, denotes that you will lead a peaceful life. **576**

ORGAN LESSON—To dream of taking organ lessons, denotes a peaceful mind. **500**

ORPHAN—Denotes lost hopes, and poverty. **473**

OSTRICH—To dream of an ostrich, denotes that you will rise far above your present position, and be happy for the remainder of your life| **555**

OTTOMAN—To sit on one, denotes busines success. **573**

OUTLAW—To dream of one of these fellows, denotes sadness and discomfort. **714**

OVEN—To dream of a hot oven denotes a pleasant surprise. **144**
A cold oven denotes sad news. **569**

OVERALLS— To dream of wearing a pair of overalls denotes that you will rise far above your present position by perseverance and sound integrity. **147**

OVERCOAT—To dream of an overcoat, denotes that you will hold your present position longer than you expect. **357**

OVERFLOW—To see anything overflow, denotes excessive pleasure, in which drinking is included. **150**

OVERPAID—To dream that you are overpaid, denotes sudden wealth. **223**

OWL—To dream of an owl, denotes that what you have done in the dark, will be brought to light. **413**

OX—To dream of an ox is a sign of dignity and power. It also denotes that you are extremely healthy. **600**

OYSTERS—To dream of eating oysters, denote a sudden marriage. **211**

To see and not touch them, indicate a reverse in business. **366**

PACKING—To dream of packing anything, denotes that you will fall heir to a legacy, left to you by a relative. **291**

To see others packing, denotes that you will lose a little money. **541**

PACKAGE—To receive a large package, denotes that you will succeed, where you least expected. **345**

To mail a package, denotes a successful career. **356**

PAD—To dream of a pad, denotes that you will be very successful in games of chances. **536**

PADDLE—To paddle in clear water, denotes success; to paddle in foul water, denotes failure. **193**

PADLOCK—To dream of a padlock, denotes that you will conduct an illegitimate business, from which you will become very prosperous. **296**

PAIL—To see a filled pail, denotes great business success, and empty pail denotes loss. **349**

PAINT—To dream of paint denotes a change of address, which will be to your utmost satisfaction. **222**

PAINTER—To dream of a painter, denotes that you

will own a beautiful house in your community
in the near future. **231**

PAJAMAS—To dream of seeing any one, in pajamas,
denotes that you will receive a declaration of love
from your sweetheart. **673**

To dream that you are dressed in pajamas, denotes
that you are living a fascinating life. **419**

PALACE—To visit one, denotes that you will invest
in a profitable business. **144**

To be driven away from a palace, denotes scorn.**580**

PALLBEARER—Denotes a successful journey. **393**

PALM TREE—To dream of one signifies that you are
keeping company with a person of questionable
character. **682**

To sit under one, denotes good health and success in
all of your adventures. **983**

PAMPHLETS—To dream of distributing any kind
of pamphlets, denote that you will be a leader of
a great cause. **271**

PANCAKES—To eat them denote good luck on the
following day. **510**

To turn away from them, is a sign of poverty and
remorse. **917**

PAPER—To dream of paper, denotes security in business. **315**

To paper your home, denotes that you will increase
your earning capacity through your steadfastness
of purpose. **329**

PAPER MONEY—Denotes great sucecss on the fol-
owing day. **567**

PARACHUTE—To dream of a parachute, denotes that
you are a lion-hearted person, and for this reason,
you are going to succeed in all of your undertakings. **287**

PARADE—To dream of a parade, denotes that you
will be called upon to manage an important organ-

ization. This position will not only make you honorable, but you wll also be wealthy. **194**

PARENTS—To dream of your parents, denote long life and much happiness. **540**

PARALYZE—To see a paralyzed person, denotes that you will receive a slight injury, which will be the direct result of your own carelessness. **564**
To dream that you are paralyzed, denotes that some one is trying to ruin your reputation. **549**

PARASOL.—To dream of a parasol, signifies financia' aid. **197**

PARK—To be in a park, denotes unrequieted love. Do not waste your time on that silly person. **276**

PARLOR—To sit in your parlor, denotes a peaceful mind. **541**
To see others in your parlor, denotes that you will have a social function soon. **317**

PAROLE—To see any one on parole, denotes that the prisoner will be pardoned. **354**

PARQUET FLOOR—To dream of this special kind of floor, denotes that you will reach the great heights and attain success. **195**

PARROT—To dream of one, denotes that you will come in contact with a stupid person. **443**

PARTNER—To dream of your partner, denotes losses. If you have a partner, watch him. That rascal is about to rob you. **387**

PASS BOOK—To dream of a passbook, denotes steady employment. **757**

PASSENGERS—To see a great deal of passengers in your sleep, denotes that you will be very successful in a strange city. **395**

PASSPORT—To own a passport, denotes that you will take a pleasant trip shortly. **346**

PASSWORD—To dream of possessing a password signifies that you will succeed in keeping a secret, which means much to you. **597**

PASTOR—To dream of a pastor, denotes business success. **839**

PASTRY—To dream of pastry, denotes ill health. **681**

PASTURE—To see one in your sleep, denotes that you will take a new grip on life. It promises a brilliant future. **616**

PATCH OF GRASS—To see a patch of grass, denotes that you will own a vast amount of property in the near future. **184**

PATENT—To dream that you have a patent on any article denotes that you will become prosperous and happy, as the years roll on. **976**

PATRIOT—To dream of one, denotes that you are a lovable good natured person, dignified in every respect. **018**

PATROL WAGON—To dream of one denotes misery and ill health. **274**

PATTERN—To dream of any kind of a pattern denotes an honorable career. **743**

PAVEMENT—To walk on a hard pavement denotes an honorable career. **743**

PAWN—To pawn anything, denotes poverty and vexation. **167**

PAWNBROKER—To see one in your sleep, denotes that you are being robbed out of your labor. **313**

PAWNSHOP—To visit one, denotes grief. **364**

PAY—To dream of receiving your pay, denotes joy and much profit. It also denotes an increase in salary. **377**

PEACH—To eat a sweet peach, denotes that you will be in love shortly. **369**
To eat a sour peach, signifies that your love will be rejected. **644**

PEACHES—Denotes a profitable marriage. **692**
To eat them signify sudden wealth. **598**

To give them away denotes a peaceful mind. **260**

PEACOCK—To see one denotes poor business transaction. **419**

PEANUTS—To eat them, denote misfortune. **768**

To turn away from them, denote that you will overthrow a dangerous enemy. **050**

PEDDLER—To dream of one denote that you will save a great deal of money from your present earnings. **616**

PEELING POTATOES—To dream of peeling potatoes, denote that you will be a servant all the days of your life. **373**

PEARS—To see a great deal of ripe pears in your sleep, signify that you will succeed in putting across an important program, which will be the turning point of your life. **196**

Young pears denote cheating. **567**

PEARLS—To dream of pearls, denote a glorious time. This is an excellent dream to lovers, as it promises success in courtship. **556**

PEBBLESTONE—To dream that your path is paved with pebblestones, denotes that you will soon realize your hopes. **326**

PECK—To dream of one denotes a death, generally a relative or friend. **772**

PEEPING—To dream of peeping at any one, denotes that you will be drawn into a plot, in which you will escape punishment, after a great deal of trouble and anxiety. **288**

PEN—To dream of a pen denotes a successful career. **111**

To dream that your pen will not write indicates failure. **311**

A gold pen is a sign of approaching marriage. **911**

PENSION—To dream of receiving a pension, denotes long life and much prosperity. **234**

PEPPER—To dream of pepper denotes that you will come in contact with a hot-headed person. **559**

PEPPERMINT—To dream of peppermint, denotes a bad cold and stomack disorders. **137**

PERCOLATOR—To dream of a percolator, denotes that you are about to attain financial success. **372**

PERFUME—To see a great deal of perfume, denotes that you will marry a wealthy person soon. Your wedding will be the talk of the town. On account of this marriage, you will leap into society, and become one of the elites. **294**

PERMIT—To dream of having any kind of a permit, denotes a profitable investment. **293**

PERSPIRE—To perspire a great deal, denotes a weak mind, but a good character. **347**
To see others perspire denotes that you will rise to power and eminence by the downfall of another person. **544**

PERSECUTION—To dream that you are being persecuted is a sign of remorse. **831**

PETTICOAT—To dream of a petticoat, denotes an abundance of pleasure. **518**
If a man dreams that his wife is wearing a short petticoat, denotes that she is unfaithful to him. She loves some one else. **542**

PHILOSOPHER—To dream of one denotes great learning. **891**

PHONOGRAPH—To hear one play, denotes a peaceful mind and happy married life. **206**

PHOTOGRAPH—To dream of your photograph, denotes that you will enter some kind of a contest. **467**
To see the photograph of another, denotes that some one is greatly opposed to you. **565**

PHYSIC—To take a physic, denotes slander and contempt. **226**

PHYSICIAN—To see one in your sleep, denotes that you will regain your health after a few months of anxiety. **343**

PIANO—To play one yourself denotes joy and much profit. **590**
To hear one play by another person, denotes sad news and lost hopes. **246**

PICTURE—To dream of a picture, denotes excellent health and good fortune. **183**

PICK-AX—To dream of using one, denotes hard work, but good pay. **362**

PICK COTTON—To dream of picking cotton is a sign of wealth and material success. **385**

PICKLES—To eat them signify that you will be called upon to perform an important task in the behalfs of mankind. **641**
To sell them is a sign of courage. **441**

PICK POCKET—To dream of a pick-pocket, denotes that you will foul your enemies at their own game. **071**

PIES—To dream of eating pies, denote sudden wealth and much happiness. **101**
To give them away denote courage and popularity. **191**

PIER—To dream of a pier, denotes a pleasant voyage. **339**

PIG—Denotes laziness. **571**

PIG-TAILS—To eat them signify happiness and wealth. **327**

PIGEON—To dream of a pigeon, denotes that you will receive a letter which will contain very good news. This is truly, an excellent dream, especially to business and professional men. **423**

PILLS—To dream of taking pills, denote that you will lose confidence in one whom you have always trusted. **345**

PILLOWS—To see many pillows in your sleep, denote romance of the highest order. 287

PILOT—To see one, denotes a rise in position. 421

PIN—To dream of a pin denotes that you are a hot tempered person, when provoked. 725

PINEAPPLES—To eat pineapples, denote long life and much happiness. 793

PINE TREE—Denotes prosperity and good health. 668

PINK DRESS—To wear one denotes that you will meet a person, who will propose marriage to you. To a married person it signifies felicity and prosperity. 444

PIN CUSHION—To see one in your sleep denotes flirtation and scandal. 201

PIPE—To dream of smoking a pipe, denotes a peaceful mind. 265
To see others smoke, is a sign of approaching marriage. 569

PISTOL—To see one in your sleep, denotes danger from an unexpected source. 173
To dream that some one points a pistol at you denotes that your enemies are too strong for you. If however you are able to take away the pistol, it denotes that you will triumph over all your enemies. 511

PITCHER—A filled pitcher denotes joy and profit. 184
An empty one, denotes that you are a keen thinker, and a great philosopher of human frailities. 367

PLAGUE—To dream of being afflicted with any kind of a plague denotes hardship for a while. 862
To see others afflicted, denotes that you will rise to a higher position in life and you will enjoy a great deal of happiness and prosperity. 910

PLANET—To dream of some heavenly planet denotes that you will discover something that will be of relative importance to you. **606**

PLANK—To dream of a plank, denotes hard work but good pay. **208**

PLANTATION—To work on one, denotes that you will live to a ripe old age, but that you will never be rich, yet you will always be able to supply your daily wants. **772**

PLANTER—To dream of a planter, denotes business success. **229**

PLASTER—Denotes that your friends are faithful. **269**

PLATE—A filled plate denotes gain, an empty one denotes losses. **139**

PLATFORM—Denotes elevation in life. **266**
To lecture from a platform denotes that you have the right idea about life in general. **260**

PLAYING BALL—To dream of playing ball is a sign of content. **901**
To see others play ball denotes a pleasant trip. **920**

PLAYING CARDS—To play cards in your sleep, denote a peaceful mind. It also denotes great success in games of chances. **203**

PLAYING DICE—Denotes good luck in all games. **711**

PLOUGH—To dream of a plough, denotes that you wll outsmart your opponent. It also signify a successful career. **185**

PLUMS—To dream of ripe plums, signify love, health

PLUM PUDDING—To dream of plum pudding denotes that you are going to have a wonderful time among friends or relatives. **266**
To make one denotes great success in business. **110**
and wealth. **281**
To eat young plums denote that you will commit a disgraceful act. **065**

PLUMBER—To dream of a plumber, denotes that you will have a poor chance in owning properties and to be benefited by them. **321**

PNEUMONIA—To have an attack of pneumonia, denotes that you are surrounded by treacherous enemies. **606**

POCKET—A filled pocket denotes good luck on the following day; an empty one, denotes lawsuits. **280**

POCKETBOOK—To find one denotes, sudden wealth. **532**

To lose one, denotes secret sorrows. **153**
To dream that someone snatches your pockebook, denotes that you are in danger of being molested by an outrageous person. **507**

POCKETKNIFE—To carry one, denotes that your liberty is in danger. **144**

POEM—To read one denotes that you will discover something of relative importance to your welfare. **666**

POET—To talk to one, mark his words in order to be benefited by them. **321**

To quarrel with a poet, denotes that you will act as decoy in a robbery. **318**

POISON—To dream of poison, denotes grief and vexation. **263**

POKER—To play poker, denotes that you will live to a ripe old age. **111**

To see others playing this game, denotes that you will succeed in obtaining a loan, where you least expected. **956**

POLICE OFFICER—Denotes an honorable career. **367**

POLICY—To dream of playing policy, signifies sudden wealth accompanied by the picture of good health. **632**

POLISH—To dream of polishing anything denotes a brilliant future. **526**

To buy polish is a sign of approaching marriage. **526**

POLITICIAN—To dream of a politician, denotes that you will have to pay some kind of a graft in order to succeed in your present undertakings. **368**

PONY—To dream of a pony, denotes good luck in games of chances. **725**

POOL—To dream of a pool of clear water, denotes great strength and much success. **389**

A pool of foul water, denotes failure and unhappiness. **437**

POOL ROOM—To visit one, denotes a wasted life. **465**

POORHOUSE—To visit one, denotes shame and remorse. **717**

POP CORN—To eat pop corn, denotes that you will be invited to go to a picnic. **271**

PORK—To eat it denotes loss of health. **428**

To give it away is a sign of shrewd business enterprise. **582**

To sell it is a sign of eloquence. **510**

PORTER—To dream of a porter, denotes that you will become very prosperous in the future. **611**

To give a tip to a porter, denotes good circumstances. It also indicates long life and much happiness. **568**

POST CARD—To send a post card to any one, denotes business success. **116**

To receive one, is a sign of great popularity. **292**

POSTMAN—Denotes that you will build up an elaborate mail order business in the near future. **493**

POST OFFICE—To dream of one denotes a very prosperous life. It also denotes long life and good health. **305**

POT—A filled pot denotes an increase in family. **155**
An empty pot, denotes sorrow and hardship. **568**

POTATOES—Cooked potatoes denote that you are about to be married to a beautiful person. **914**
Raw potatoes denote an unfortunate marriage. **143**

POWDER—To see gun powder in your sleep denotes quarrel and dissatisfaction. **536**
To dream of face powder denotes that you will acquire a set of beautiful clothes in the future. **267**
To powder your face, denotes that you are becoming more beautiful than ever. **367**

PREGNANCY—If a woman dreams that she is pregnant; it is a sure sign that she will be delivered of a beautiful baby boy in the near future. **183**

PRESIDENT—To dream of the president, denotes that you will get a good position shortly. From this position you will realize a decent sum of money, which you will invest successfully. **444**

PRETTY—To see anything that is pretty is a sign of ambition and self perseverance. **322**

PRINCE—To talk to one, denotes great popularity. It also denotes success. **511**

PRINCESS—To dream of a princess, denotes that you will visit an unusual place. **283**

PRINCIPAL—To dream of a principal of a school or college, denotes that you will rise far above your present position in life and be happy. **379**

PRINTER—To dream of a printer, denotes that you will attend a celebrated social function. **644**

PRISON—To be confined in one denotes lost hopes. **237**
To leave one denotes that you will receive a letter, the contents of which, will cause you to be overjoyed. **412**

PRIZE—To be the recipient of a prize denotes that a dark cloud is about to pass over your life; after that you will be prosperous and happy. **224**

PRIZE FIGHTER—To see one in your sleep, denotes that you will triumph over your enemies to such an extent, that they will try to gain your good will. **673**

PROCESSION—To witness one, denotes a wedding. **749**

PROPERTY—To dream of buying or acquiring property in any way denotes a prosperous life. **415** To sell property is a sign of peace and satisfaction. **516**

PUPIL—To dream that you are a pupil, denotes great popularity. **401**

PUMPKINS—Denotes an increase in family. You will have a great many sons and daughters, all of whom will be the pride of your old age. **851**

PUNISHMENT—To dream that you are being punished, denotes slander and notoriety. **293** To see others being punished, denotes that you will put your enemies to flight. **590**

PUGILIST—To see one in your sleep indicates popularity. **595**

PULLEY—To dream of a pulley, denotes that you are mechanically inclined. **277**

PULPIT—Denotes eloquence and good fortune. **225**

PROPOSE—To dream that some one proposes marriage to you, denotes joy and much happiness. **262**

PROSTITUTE—To dream of a prostitute, denotes a dangerous disease. This is a warning of sickness. **135**

PRUNES—Denote steady employment. **557**

PSALMS—To dream of chanting the psalms of David, denotes that you will put your enemies to flight by using keen judgment. **219**

PUDDING—To see a great deal of pudding in your sleep, denotes that you are about to succeed in your undertakings. **101**

PUZZLE—To dream that you are being puzzled in
your sleep, denotes that you will have a great
deal of difficulty in collecting a certain sum of
money. **397**

To work out a cross word puzzle, denotes joy and
profit. **525**

PYRAMID—To dream of a pyramid, denotes an increase of knowledge. **172**

QUACK DOCTOR—To have one attend you, denotes
that you will save a great deal of money through
economy and thrift. **363**

QUAKER OATS—To dream of Quaker oats, denotes a good appetite, and the picture of good
health. **786**

QUARRELING—To dream of quarreling, denotes
great friendship and content. **533**

QUARRY—To work in one, denotes that you will do
a great favor to one in need. You will be greatly
rewarded for this kindness in times to come. **591**

QUART OF BEER—To dream of a quart of beer, denotes that you will become a bootlegger in the
near future. You will acquire a decent sum of
money from this business. **291**

QUASH—To see a great deal of quash, denotes good
crops to farmers. To others it denotes a successful career. **511**

QUEEN—To see one in your sleep, denotes that you
will command wealth and popularity in the near
future. **720**

To quarrel with a queen, signifies loss of position.
608

QUESTION—To dream that you are being questioned,
denotes that you will be engaged in a law suit,
in which you will overthrow your opponent. **655**

QUESTIONAIRE—To answer a question, denotes

that you will succeed in obtaining a government position. **473**

If you are unable to answer the questionaire, it is a sure sign of business failures. **077**

QUICKLIME—To see a great deal of quicksilver denotes that you are well protected from danger. **728**

QUICKSAND—Denotes that you are being slandered by one who visits you daily. Beware of that person. **781**

QUICKSILVER—Is a sign of steady employment. **671**

QUILT—To dream of a bed quilt, denotes everlasting prosperity accompanied by the picture of good health. **187**

QUIT—To dream that you quit your place of employment, denotes that you will be persuaded to commit an act of injustice. **684**

QUININE—Denotes sickness. **510**

To see others take quinine, denotes that you will come in contact with a stupid person who brags a great deal. **545**

RABBI—To talk to one, denotes a long life, filled with peace and satisfaction. **325**

To quarrel with one, denotes loss of ambition. **599**

RABBIT—To see a rabbit denotes wealth and much happiness. **101**

To eat a rabbit denotes joy and profit. **510**

To kill a rabbit, denotes injustice to a friend. **540**

RABBIT'S FOOT—To carry a rabbit's foot, denotes honorable and successful career. It denotes that everything is coming your way. **543**

RACE—To run a race on foot, denotes good luck on the following day. All other races, denote an honorable career. **717**

RACE HORSE—To dream of a race horse, denotes that you will be very successful in games of chances. Your number will show up soon. It is up to you now, after having this wonderful dream. **736**

RACOON—Denotes a change of employment for the better. **216**

RADIO—To hear one play, denotes long life and much happiness. **110**

RADIOPHONE—To dream of a radiophone, denotes excessive pleasure. That pleasure no one knows. **224**

RAFFLE—To partake in a raffle, denotes great success in salesmanship. **256**

To dream that you are the conductor of the raffle denotes that you will try to obtain money by dishonest means. **539**

RAFT—To be adrift on one denotes wealth and happiness. **114**

To see others adrift on a raft denotes that the prisoner will be acquitted for the lack of evidence. **154**

RAGGED—To see a ragged person, denotes that you will be sorry for acting too hastily on a particular affair. **192**

To dream that you are dressed in rags, denotes loneliness. **579**

RAGTIME—To hear ragtime music, denotes joy to your heart's content. It also indicates a prosperous and happy existence. **237**

RAILING—To dream that your home is surrounded by a railing, denotes domestic tranquility, and a reunion among friends. **144**

RAIN—To dream that it rains, denotes a good crop to farmers. To others it is a sign of financial success. **271**

RAINBOW—Denotes sunshine, and success in love affairs. **691**

RAINCOAT—To wear one, denotes business security,

and an increase in fortune. **379**

RAILROAD—To dream of a railway denotes steady employment. **114**

RAISONS—Denotes, health, wealth and happiness. **763**

RAM GOAT—Denotes sudden wealth. This is a good omen for business people. **092**

RANCH—To visit one, denotes that you will succeed in obtaining the position that you now desire. **361**

RATTLE SNAKE—Denotes sickness. **362**

RASPBERRY—To dream of raspberry, denotes that you are wasting your time and money on some one, who does not deserve your kind attention. **539**

RAT—To see one, denotes good luck on the following day. **732**

RATTLE SNAKE—Denotes a dirty disease. **546**

RAZOR—To dream of a razor denotes discrimination. It also denotes strife and vexation. **694**

RAZOR STROP—To dream of a razor strop, denotes good luck in business. **840**

READING—To read a letter, denotes business success. **541**
To read a newspaper denotes domestic tranquility. **417**
To read a book denotes that you will aid a friend financially. **699**

REBELLION—To dream of a rebellion, denotes trials and tribulations. **352**

RECEPTION—To dream that you attend a reception, denotes an abundance of pleasure. It also indicates that some one is going to make love to you within a few days. You are going to love this person dearly. **029**

RECITAL—To attend one, signifies prudence and popularity. To recite yourself is a sign of benevolence. **296**

RECOMMENDATION—To receive a recommendation from any one, denotes that you will hold an important position in your community on account of this position, you will become very popular. **730**

REINDEER—To dream of a reindeer, denotes that your wife or husband is unfaithful. **220**

RED TAPE—To dream of going through a great deal of red tape, signifies dishonor. **538**

REJOICE—To rejoice in your sleep, denotes a happy marriage. It also indicates loyalty. **411**

REGISTER—To see one in your sleep, denotes profitable investment. **735**

RENT—To dream of paying rent signifies profit and loss. **214**

To dream that you are unable to pay rent is a sign of arguments and discontent. **266**

REPORTER—To dream of a reporter, denotes scandal and notoriety. **514**

RESERVOIR—To dream of a reservoir denotes success in business and love affairs. **272**

RESTAURANT—To visit one, denotes that you will save a great sum of money in the near future. **321**

REVENUE OFFICER—Denotes that you will conduct a bootlegging business, from which you will become very prosperous. **673**

REVOLUTION—To dream of a revolution denotes want and misery. **512**

REVOLVER—To dream of a revolver, denotes danger from an unexpected source. **580**

RHEUMATISM—To have an attack of this sickness, denotes weakness of mind. **534**

RICE—To dream of eating rice, denotes wealth and much happiness. This is an excellent dream to gamblers. **671**

RICE PUDDING—To eat it, signifies great wealth and popularity. **487**

To see it and not to eat it, denotes failure in business at present. **321**

RICH—To dream that you are rich, when in reality you are not, is a sign of financial success. It also indicates that you will take hold of a great opportunity, which will be the turning point of your life. **752**

RIDDLE—To solve one, denotes that you possess great mental faculties. **101**

If you are unable to solve the riddle, it indicates that your opportunities will be limited. **544**

RIFLE—To dream of a rifle, denotes robbery and mischief. **277**

RINGLEADFR—To dream of a ringleader of any affair, denotes that you will cause a great deal of trouble to one that you love dearly. You will cause this trouble by speaking too hastily, for which you will regret. **728**

RIDE—To dream that you ride a powerful horse, indicates great success in business. **144**

To see others ride denote that you will invest in a good paying proposition. **563**

To fall from a horse denotes an unprofitable investment. **344**

RIOT—To see one in your sleep denotes death of a prominent person. **628**

RIVER—A river of clear water, signifies an honorable career. **543**

A river of muddy water denotes strife and ill luck. **419**

To swim in a river of clear water, denotes brilliant future. **407**

ROAD—To travel over a nice and clean road, denotes great success in business and love affairs. **673**

To travel over a dark and dusty road, is a sign of financial difficulties. **300**

A muddy road, denotes that unless you use good precaution you will be outwitted by your enemies. **509**

ROCKS—To dream of large rocks, denote great success. **316**

Small ones indicate failure. **366**

ROBBERS—To see them in your sleep, denote that you will persuade a friend to commit an act of indecency for your own benefit. **110**

ROCKET—To dream of a sky rocket, denotes an abundance of rain and good crops. **119**

ROCKING CHAIR—To sit in one, denotes a happy married life, and enjoyment among friends and relatives. **540**

To rock yourself to sleep, denotes long life and prosperity. **969**

To see a person in a rocking chair, denotes safety of your affairs. **525**

ROLL—To dream of a music roll, denotes an abundance of pleasure and good fortune. **713**

Bread rolls denote thrift and economy. **267**

ROLLING PIN—Signifies a fight between husband and wife. It also indicates grief and vexation. **362**

ROOF GARDEN—To visit one, denotes that you will receive a declaration of love from your swettheart. **510**

ROOMING HOUSE—To visit one, denotes that your wife or husband is flirting with some one else. **345**

To leave a rooming house, denotes safety of your affairs. **690**

ROOSTER—To hear one crow, denotes that someone is trying to betray you. Their efforts will be in vain, because you are a shrewd person. **331**

To kill one, denotes skill and ambition. **569**

ROPE—To see one, denotes profitable business enterprises. **561**

To cut a rope, denotes that you will foul your
enemies. **693**

To admire a rope dancer, denotes that some one is
deep in love with you. **769**

ROSES—To dream of roses is a sign of approaching
marriage. To those who are already married, it
denotes extreme good fortune and domestic happiness. **368**

ROSE WATER—To dream of rose water, denotes
that you are going to do a great deal of baking in
the near future. You are going to make pastries
of all kinds. **290**

ROTTEN—To dream of anything rotten is a token of
loss. **251**

ROUND TABLE—To dream of a round table, warns
you not to disclose your secret to any one. If
you do it will bring about your downfall. **114**

ROWBOAT—To dream of a rowboat, denotes a pleasant vacation. **518**

RUBBER—To dream of any kind of rubber, denotes
protection and safety of your affairs. **500**

RUDDER—To see one, denotes a successful sea voyage. **518**

RUG—To dream of a new rug, denotes that you will
meet your future wife or husband at a social gathering some time this season. Your marriage will be
one of great success. **671**

RUN—To run denotes safety of your affairs. **767**

To run to catch a train, denotes profitable employment. **144**

To run through a corn field, denotes good crops to
farmers; to others it denotes success in business.
567

To run to catch a boat denotes that you are wasting profitable time. **679**

RUNAWAY—To see a runaway, denotes lost hopes. **516**

RUPTURE—Denotes sickness and grief. **844**

RUSH—To dream that you are in a hurry, denotes grief and vexation. **711**

RYE—To dream of rye, denotes an abundance of wealth and happiness. **291**

SACK—To carry a heavy sack, denotes that you will get a politician's job. **691**

To carry an empty sack, denotes sad memories. **540**

SACRAMENT—To take sacrament, denotes that you will go into the world to win souls. Your mission will be one of praise worthiness. **566**

SADDLE—To see one, denotes a speedy journny. **514**

To saddle a horse, denotes that you will be employed by a wealthy person or concern in the near future. **276**

SAFE—To see one, denotes business success. **544**

To crack one, denotes great skill and popularity. **444**

SAGO—To drink sago, denotes an excellent investment. **158**

SAILING—To dream of sailing in nice weather denotes security in all kinds of business. It also indicates the picture of good health. **715**

To sail in rough weather is a sign of loss and contempt. **710**

SAILOR—To dream of a sailor, denotes that you will succeed in evading a dangerous character. **541**

To see many sailors at work, denotes a pleasant voyage. **167**

SALAD—Denotes domestic tranquility and great wealth. **619**

SALARY—To dream that your salary is being raised,

denotes joy and much happiness. It also indicates some wealth. **449**

To dream that your salary has been reduced, is an evil omen. **529**

SALESMAN—To see one, denotes that some one will persuade you to invest in a questionable enterprise. **229**

SALE—To attend one denotes great success in business. **443**

SALMON—To eat it, denotes that you are being loved by a beautiful girl. **541**

To a young woman she will meet a man who will propose marriage to her at first sight. **641**

SALOON—To enter one, denotes a prosperous married life. **777**

To drink in a saloon, denotes dishonor. **490**

SALT—Denotes sad news and misfortune. **386**

SALVATION ARMY—To dream of this patriotic society, denotes that you will succeed in obtaining charity, either from the government, or from some other organized society. **144**

To dream that you are a member of the Salvation army, denotes success in love and business affairs. **084**

SAND—To dream of sand, denotes that you will have a great many children. Some of them will become school teachers, doctors, and lawyers. **381**

SAND PAPER—To use or see a great deal of sand paper, denotes a secret marriage. **438**

SANDWICH—To eat a sandwich, denotes poor health. This dream warns you to look after your health. **711**

SAPPHIRE—This dream denotes cunning enemies, and dangerous pleasure. **440**

SARDINE—To see a great deal of sardines, denote that you will be surrounded by sincere friends in the near future. **732**

To eat sardines, denotes luck in games of chances. **539**

SATAN—To see this evil fellow, denotes great temptation, but an abundance of pleasure. **531**

To be able to chase him away, denotes a successful career. **062**

SAUERKRAUT—To dream of sauerkraut signifies poor advice from one who means well. **091**

SAUSAGE—To eat sausage denotes a lonely life. **560**

To throw it away, denotes a favorable investment. **369**

To buy it denotes scandal. **566**

SAVINGS BANK—To enter one, denotes that you will get a job, which will be to your utmost satisfaction. From this job, you will realize a decent sum of money, which you will invest and make more money. **387**

SAW—To dream of a saw, denotes hard work, but good pay. **672**

SAXAPHONE—To dream of one denotes annoyance and vexation. **549**

To play one yourself, denotes temptation and vexation. **498**

SCALD—To dream of scalding yourself, denotes your wishes will be realized, and that you will be happy and prosperous for the remaining of your life. **896**

To see others scald themselves denotes deception. **512**

SCALES—To dream of a pair of scales, denotes that you will be justified in acting in a certain way. **148**

SCALP—To dream of seeing any one's scalp denotes disappointment and failure in executing your plans. **207**

SCAFFOLD—To see one in your sleep is a sure sign of dishonor. This dream warns you to be more dignified in the manner in which you are now living. **479**

SCARF—To wear one, denotes that your sweetheart is true to you. **119**

SCARS—To dream of having many scars, indicates a dangerous and unprofitable undertaking. **000**

SCHOLAR—To dream of a scholar, denotes success in all kinds of business on the following day. **198**

SCHOOL—To visit one, denotes that you will be refreshed by the sweet memories of by gone days. It also indicates much profit. **143**

SCHOOL MASTER—To dream of one, denotes that you should follow your own mind in dealing with the problem that you now have in hand. Take advice from no one. **143**

SCHOOLMISTRESS—Denotes an honorable and successful career. **431**

SCHOONER—To see one sailing denotes joy and profit. **442**
A still schooner, denotes you are losing valuable time. **691**

SCISSORS—To use one, signifies a loving partner and many dutiful children. **592**
To buy a pair of scissors, denotes small earnings. **760**

SCOLD—To scold any one denotes that you are a broad-minded person. **932**
To dream that you are being scolded by another person is a sign of weakness on your part to execute your plans. **896**

SCORN—To scorn any one, signifies that someone will tell a lie on you, in order to shield himself. **519**

SCORPION—Denotes a dangerous and malicious

enemy. **549**

To kill a scorpion, denotes that you will triumph over your enemies. **375**

SCOTCHMAN—To dream of one, denotes that some one, will tell a funny joke about another person. **218**

SCREAM—To dream that you scream in your sleep, denotes a great deal of pleasure. **161**

To hear others scream, signifies opposition and contention. **426**

SCREW DRIVER—To use one, denotes that you will purchase an automobile in the near future. **276**

SCRIPTURES—To dream of reading the scriptures denotes a comfortable married life, accompanied by many dutiful and handsome children, generally three boys and two girls. **506**

SCRUBBING—To dream of scrubbing, signifies ordinary circumstances. **139**

SEA—A smooth sea is a sign of happiness accompanied by an abundance of wealth. **481**

A rough sea denotes a controversy with friends or relatives. **274**

SEA MONSTER—To see one is a sign of prosperity and assimilation among friends. **287**

SEA PLANE—To dream of a sea plane, denotes that a sincere friend has lost your address, and is trying with all endeavor to locate you. **229**.

SEAL—To see one in your sleep denotes a successful adventure which will not only bring you fame, but wealth also. **008**

SEARCH—To search for anything, denotes grief and vexation. **132**

If you are unable to find what you are searching for, is a sign of great disappointment. **365**

SEARCHLIGHT—To use a searchlight, denotes that you will discover a startling truth. **394**

To see others using a searchlight, signifies prosperity. **393**

SEASHORE—To be at the seashore, denotes a happy reunion among friends and relatives. **519**

SEPULCHRE—To dream of a sepulchre that you will visit a scene of historical background. **150**

SERMON—To hear a sermon, denotes a peaceful mind. **400**

To preach yourself, denotes great popularity. **541**

SERVANT—To dream that you are a servant, denotes that you will receive a humble and yet an honorable position. **781**

To see many servants at work, denotes that you will marry a servant girl. **561**

To a young woman it is a sign of love affairs. **544**

SEWING MACHINE—Denotes that you will accumulate wealth slowly. **091**

SEXTON—To dream of a sexton, denotes a baptism. **547**

SHARKS—Denotes cunning and dangerous enemies. **397**

SHAVE—To be shaved by a barber denotes a successful career. **721**

To shave yourself denotes success in trade and industry. **385**

SHAWL—To wear one, denotes business success. **157**

A shawl of many colors, signifies that you are wasting your talent. **576**

SHEEP—To dream of a great number of sheep, denote that you will be led astray, by one whom you have always trusted. **963**

To attend a number of sheep, is a sign of everlasting prosperity. **549**

SHEET—Denotes perpetual happiness. **637**

SHELL—To dream of an empty shell denotes that you will receive unpleasant news. This news however, will prove to be untrue. 011

SHELL SHOCK—To see a shell shock person, denotes that you will cause much trouble to a friend, which will be unintentional on your part. 186

SHERIFF—To dream of a sheriff denotes that you will receive a dispossess. 569

SHINGLES—To dream of shingles is a sign that you will purchase a beautiful home shortly. 511

SHIP—To see one, sailing on a smooth sea, denotes profitable investments. 368

To see one sailing in bad weather, denotes lost hope. 069

To see a ship of weather beaten sailors, is a token of remorse. 655

To dream of a shipwreck, denotes failure in business. 699

SHIPYARD—To work in one, denotes a job of long hours, but good pay. 532

SHIPWRECK—To dream of being shipwrecked denotes a dangerous undertaking. 747

To dream that you are able to reach land safely after being shipwrecked denotes triumph over your enemies. 673

SHIRT—A clean shirt denotes prosperity; a soiled one, is a sign of remorse. 583

SHOES—New shoes denote a blessing; old ones signify lost hopes. 444

SHOEMAKER—To see one at work denotes good luck and extraordinary good health. 304

To have one mend your shoes, denotes that you will acquire a host of new friends, who will aid you in time of want. 369

SHOOT—To dream that some one shoots at you, denotes unseen danger. 427

To shoot at any one, denotes grief and vexation, this is a evil omen. 117

SHOPKEEPER—To see one in your sleep, denotes contention. 192

To quarrel with one denotes popularity. 519

SHOPPING—To dream of going shopping, denotes prosperity and happiness. 306

To see others shop signifies joy and jollity. 005

SHOVEL—Denotes grief and vexation. 514

SHOWBOAT—To visit a showboat, denotes that you will succeed in getting an expensive winter coat this season. You will be the talk of the town. 544

SHOWROOM—To visit a showroom, denotes that you will marry the person to whom you are now engaged; your marriage will be one of great success. 417

SHRIMPS—To eat them, denotes that you will establish a good paying business. 575

To turn away from them denotes deceit and treachery. 634

SICK—To see a sick person denotes ill health to the dreamer. 416

SIDEWALKS—To traverse the sidewalks of New York denote popularity and success in business. It also indicates good luck in games of chances. 736

To be strolling on the sidewalks of Michigan, is a sign of great wealth. 932

The sidewalks of Pittsburgh denote profit and pleasure. 962

To be on the sidewalks of Monte Carlo, denotes that you will win a large sum of money on the following day. 365

The sidewalks of Paris, denote success in love. It also indicates a passionate marriage. 362

To be on the sidewalks of Berlin, denote profitable and stable investments. 500

To be on the sidewalks of Hong Kong, China, denote domestic tranquility and perpetual opportunities. 611

To traverse the sidewalks of London, England is a sign of power and riches in abundance. **327**

SIEVE—To dream of one denotes that your sweetheart is untrue to you. **114**

SIGHT—To dream of losing your sight denotes loss of ambition and prestige. **733**

SILK—To dream of an abundance of silk, denotes that you will be the recipient of an expensive gift. Generally a gift from your lover. **796**

To wear silk clothing, denotes much happiness and everlasting prosperity. **601**

SISTER—To dream of your sister, denotes that you will be persuaded to make up with one with whom you had a misunderstanding. **725**

SILVER—Is a sure sign of disappointment. **139**

SING—To sing yourself denotes peace and prosperity. **540**

To hear others sing, signifies moderate circumstances. **967**

SIREN—To hear one, denotes that your enemy will be cast into prison. **248**

SKATING RINK—To dream of visiting one is a sign of riches and amusements to your heart's content. **893**

SKELETON—To see a skeleton in your sleep denotes troubles and vexation. **782**

SKIPPING—To dream of skipping signifies the speedy return of your lover. Your difference will be duly compromised, and everything is going to work out to your utmost satisfaction. **425**

SKULL—To see many skulls denote danger and anger. **422**

SKY—To see a clear sky denotes wealth and happiness. **122**

To see dark clouds signify grief and dishonor. **223**
Red skies indicate misfortune. **821**

SLACKER—To dream of a slacker denotes that you are wasting your money and time on one who does not deserve it. **362**

SLAUGHTER HOUSE—Denotes that you will succeed in obtaining your wishes. **041**

SLEDGE—To use one, denotes hard work but excellent pay. **194**

SLEEP—To sleep with one of the opposite sex, signifies happiness and much wealth. **391**
To sleep with a handsome person, denotes joy and profit. To sleep with a homely person denotes grief and vexation. **315**

SLEIGHING—To dream of sleighing denotes, an abundance of pleasure. It also indicates success in love affairs. **949**

SLIPPERS—To wear slippers denote that you will marry. Your marriage will be one of everlasting peace and prosperity. **673**

SLOT MACHINE—To operate one, denotes loss in games of chances. **739**

SMALL POX—To dream of seeing any one, with this malady, denotes that one, of your friends is suffering from a terrible disease. **639**

SMELLING SALTS—To dream of using smelling salts, denotes an unpleasant trip. **544**

SMOCK—If a woman dreams of wearing a smock, it denotes that she will be pregnant soon. **191**

SMOKE—To dream of a great deal of smoke, denotes that you will be heavily insured in the near future. **187**
To see smoke and no fire denotes danger from an unexpected source. **591**

SMUGGLERS—To see a great many smugglers in your sleep. denotes that one of your friends will persuade you to commit an act of injustice. **517**

SNAKE—A rattle snake denotes a disease which will cause you a great deal of money in order to be cured. **562**

SNOW—To dream of snow denotes an honorable life. **333**

SNOWBALL—To eat a snowball, denotes that you will utter words in anger, which will greatly lower your prestige and respectability. **183**

SNUFF—To take snuff, denotes content and prosperity. **336**

SOAP—To dream of bars of soap, signify that you will be highly recommended for an important position, for which you are so well fitted. **654**

SOCIALISM—To dream of socialism, denotes that you will be well paid for your services. It also denotes long life and prosperity. **235**

SOCIAL WORKER—To dream of one, denotes that you will marry a person who is tender and loving. **333**
To dream that you are a social worker, denotes an honorable and prosperous career. **656**

SODA FOUNTAIN—To see one, denotes good luck in games of chances. It also denotes easy money. **412**

SODA—To drink soda, denotes a good appetite. It is a sign of extra good health. **516**

SOFA—To sit on a sofa, denotes that you will receive a declaration of love from your sweetheart. **226**

SOLDIER—To dream of an army of soldiers, denotes a condition which will greatly change your affairs for the better. **529**

SOLITARY—To dream that you are solitary, is a sign of despondency for a little while. **305**

SOLO—To sing a solo, is a sign of great prosperity. **123**
To hear others sing a solo denotes joy and profit. **400**

SOMERSAULT—To make a somersault, denotes that your plan will be frustrated. **378**

SONG—To dream of singing or humming a song denotes cheerful news. This is a sure sign of success. **282**

SORES—Denotes riches in proportion to the amount of sores. **214**

SORROW—To be sorrowful in your sleep, denotes you will hurt another person's feeling through ignorance. **485**

SPAGHETTI—To eat spaghetti, denotes that you will try to make money by acting shrewd. **541**
To dream that you do not wish to eat it, signifies misrepresentation. **198**

SPANGLE BANNER—To hear the Spangle Banner, denotes great wealth and everlasting prosperity. This is an excellent dream to all. **278**

SPANIARD—To dream of a spaniard, denotes that you will prove your innocency without much effort. **517**

SPARERIB—To eat it, denotes a happy home, with many dutiful children. **252**

SPARROW—To see one in your sleep, denotes losses and vexation. **111**
To farmers, it denotes bad crops. **407**

SPATS—To wear spats, is a sign of prosperity accompanied by the picture of good health. **547**

SPEARMINT—To eat spearmint, is a sign of intense emotion. **111**

SPECIALISTS—To speak to one, denotes that you will come in contact with a plain, simple lovable person of good personality, and excellent character. This person will render you a great service. **616**

SPECIAL DELIVERY—Denotes great business opportunities. **197**

SPEECH—To deliver one denotes honor and dignity. **931**

To hear others deliver a speech, denotes safety of your affairs. **369**

SPEECHLESS—To dream that you are unable to talk is a sign of adversity and shame. **347**

SPECULATE—To dream that you speculate is a sign of profit and loss. **136**

SPICE—To dream of spice, denotes a successful enterprise. **610**

SPIDER—To see one in your sleep, denotes that you will receive a sum of money in a short time. **221**

SPIRITS—To dream of spirits, warn you to examine everything that you eat carefully. Some one is jealous of you on account of your welfare and intelligence. **352**

SPIT—To dream of spitting, denotes that you will suffer from indigestion shortly unless you pay more attention to your diet. **207**

SPOON—To use one, denotes a peaceful mind. **355**

SPORTSMAN—To see one in your sleep, denotes that a no count person will make love to you. **312**

To a man it is a sign of vexation. **133**

SPRING—A spring of clear water denotes an abundance of wealth and extremely good health. **345**

A spring of muddy water denotes failure. **219**

To dream of the spring of the year denotes success in love and romance. **625**

SPY—To see one denotes that your wife or husband has lost faith in you. **216**

SQUIRREL—To dream of one, denotes ordinary circumstances. **234**

STAB—To dream of being stabbed denotes grief. **516**

To stab someone denotes empty honor. **188**

STABLE—To visit one, denotes a humble marriage. **135**

STAGE—To be on the stage, denotes that you will obtain your goal. **573**

To see others performing on a stage denotes abundance of pleasure. **632**

STAIRCASE—To ascend one, denotes elevation of fortune. **711**

To descend one, denotes little hope. **369**

STAIRS—To ascend one, denotes that you will aspire to a higher position in life. **365**

To descend one, denotes disappointment. **560**

STAMMER—To dream that you stammer in your sleep denotes weakness and cowardice. **116**

To hear others stammer denotes that you will overthrow your enemies. **361**

STAMPS—To buy stamps denote big business enterprise. **524**

STAMPEDE—To witness one, denotes destruction. **187**

STARS—To dream of admiring the stars, denote a brilliant future, and a loving partner. **321**

STARCH—To dream of starch, denotes that someone whom you think is dishonest is an upright and straight-forward person of sound integrity. **536**

STATIONERY STORE—To visit one, denotes success in all your undertakings. **414**

STEAL—To dream that you steal from any one, denotes sorrow. **215**

STEAM ROLLER—To see ont at work, denotes that you will succeed in putting across a great proposition. **281**

To see one standing still, is a sign of domestic tranquility. **466**

STEAMSHIP—To sail in one, is a sign of a big business transaction, from which you will be greatly benefitted. **633**

To see one in danger of being shipwrecked is a sign

of adversity. **300**

STENOGRAPHER—To see a pretty stenographer denotes success in love affairs. It also indicates everlasting prosperity. **195**

STEPS—To sit on your own steps, denote a comfortable life. **511**

> To sit on the step of others is a sign of despondency. **600**

STEP LADDER—Denotes a successful career. **715**

> To buy one denotes a change of residence for the better. **210**

STEPFATHER—To dream of your stepfather, denotes ill treatment from your employer. **368**

STEWARD—To dream of a steward, denotes a great feast accompanied by amusements. **569**

STICK—A walking stick denotes quarrels which may lead to a fistic fight. **419**

STILLBORN BABY—To dream of a stillborn baby, denotes that you will hear news, which will shock you. **190**

STOCK EXCHANGE—To dream of the stock exchange, signifies prosperity and the picture of good health. **471**

STOCKINGS—To dream of wearing silk stockings, denote a brilliant future. It indicates good luck in all kinds of games of chances. **211**

> To dream of wearing torn or cotton stockings, is a sign of poverty. **499**

STONE—To dream of a large stone denotes success in all of your undertakings. **572**

> A small stone is a sign of business difficulties. **327**

STOOL PIGEON—To dream of one denotes temptation. **367**

STORE HOUSE—To dream of one denotes that you will receive a sum of money shortly. **323**

STORM—To dream of a storm, denotes sad news.

It also indicates a dreary and wasted life. **215**

STOVE—A hot stove denotes prosperity. **193**

A cold one, signifies good news from afar. **169**

STRAINER—To dream of a strainer, denotes that you will lead a straight and honest life from now on. **194**

STRANGE CITY—To dream of being in a strange city, denotes new and thrilling experience. **525**

STRANGER—To come in contact with a stranger in your sleep, denotes that you will succeed in acquiring the information which you are now seeking. **324**

To quarrel with the stranger, denotes lost hopes. **325**

STRAWBERRIES—To see a great deal of strawberries in your sleep, denote exceedingly good fortune. **573**

To eat them, denote joy and much profit. **672**

STREET CAR—To ride in one denotes joy and profit. **414**

STRETCHER—To see one, denotes that you will be sick for a short while; generally a cold or some other ailment. **231**

STRING BEANS—To dream of string beans, denote malice **452**

STUCCO HOUSE—Denotes that you will become very prosperous on account of your splendid education. **347**

STUDY—To study denotes wisdom and popularity. **136**

STUDENT—To dream of a student, denotes elevation and success. **694**

STRYCHNINE—Denotes danger from an unexpected source. **634**

SUBMARINE—To see one denotes grief. **364**

To see one submerge into the water denotes war. **311**

SUBWAY—To ride in the subway denotes profitable employment. **465**

SUGAR CAKE—Denotes that you will marry a very prominent and successful person. **868**

SUGAR CANES—To dream of sugar canes, denote a successful marriage accompanied by many dutiful children; generally three girls and two boys. **279**

SUGAR PLANTATION—To dream of one, denotes small wages and hard work. **569**

To work on a sugar plantation, denotes dissatisfaction. **513**

SUICIDE—To dream of a suicide, denotes that all of your efforts are in vain. **500**

SUIT—To dream of having a new suit made, denotes joy and good fortune on the following day. **387**

SUIT CASE—To pack one, denotes a pleasant journey. **312**

SULPHUR—To eat it in your food, denotes loss of ambition and self perseverance. **444**

SUMMER—To dream of summer at another time of the year, denotes great joy and prosperity. **534**

SUMMERHOUSE—To dream of a summerhouse, denotes an abundance of pleasure. **356**

SUMMONS—To receive one, denotes that some one will play a joke on you. You will be upset at first, until you realize what it is all about. **389**

SUN—To dream that the sun is shining bright, denotes a brilliant future. **368**

SUNDAY SCHOOL—To attend one, denotes that you will be comforted by the sweet memories of the past. **582**

SUPERINTENDENT—To see one in your sleep, denotes power and dignity, followed by years of good fortune. **217**

SUPPER—To dream of having supper denotes luxuries. **627**

SUPREME COURT—To dream of the Supreme Court, denotes that you will succeed in winning your case. **307**

SQUEEZE—To dream of being squeezed signifies that some one is trying to ruin your reputation, by spreading false propaganda against you. **566**

SURVEYOR—To see one, denotes that you will become a property owner in the near future. **467**

SUSPENDERS—To see them in your sleep, denote that you will be on easy street before long. **200**

SWALLOW—To dream of a swallow, denotes a mild winter. **216**

SWAMP—To be in one is a sign of humiliation. **260**

SWEAR—To dream that you swear, denotes that some one will cause you to be angry. **323**

SWEATSHOP—To work in one, denotes hardship, plenty work, and little food. **146**

SWEATER—To wear one, denotes ordinary circumstances. **564**

SWEEP—To sweep a house, denotes prosperity. **373**
To sweep the streets is a sign of discontent. **510**
To sweep a cellar, denotes that you are wasting valuable time. **619**
To sweep an old barn denotes that you will lose part of your savings. **634**

SWEEPSTAKE—To dream of a sweepstake ticket denotes that you will win a sum of money shortly. **673**

SWEETBREAD—To eat a great deal of sweetbread, denotes wealth and much happiness. **543**

SWEETHEART—To dream that your sweetheart holds you in his arms and whispers funny things into your ear, denotes joy and everlasting prosperity. **417**
To see him walking or flirting with some one else, denotes a misunderstanding and contempt. **700**

SWEET BISCUIT—To eat them is a sign of riches accompanied by good health. It also indicates good luck in all kinds of games of chances. **464**

SWEET OIL—Denotes faithful friends. **357**

SWEET POTATOES—To dream of sweet potatoes denote a marriage for wealth and not love. **765**

SWIM—To swim in clear water, denotes success. **543**
   To swim in muddy water denotes failure. **409**

SWING—To see any one swinging, denotes good fortune. **182**
   To swing yourself, denotes a change of address for the better. **449**

SWITCHBOARD OPERATOR—Denotes laziness. **316**

SWORD—To see one in your sleep denotes prominence and prosperity. **567**
   To cut any one with a sword indicates trouble. **617**

SYCAMORE TREE—Denotes success in love affairs. **418**

SYRINGE—To dream of a syringe, denotes that you are an intelligent person. On account of this, you will succeed in all of your undertakings. **735**

SYRUP—To drink it, denotes good fortune and everlasting prosperity. It also indicates excellent health. **760**

TABERNACLE—To visit one signifies that you are about to change your place of worship. **245**

TABLE—To dream of a table denotes a great feast and amusements. **141**
   A rund table denotes that you will attend an important conference. **519**

TACKS—To see them denote trouble and anxiety. **643**

TADPOLE—To dream of a tadpole denotes great learning. It also indicates that you possess unlimited powers and self perseverance. **563**

TAIL—To dream of having a long tail denotes peril to those who are working on dangerous jobs. **669**

To see others with a tail denotes loss of appetite. **610**

TAILOR—To see one, denotes that you will be prosperous and happy in the near future. **493**

TAKING MEDICINE—Denotes sunshine and sorrow. **543**

TAMBOURINE—To shake one, denotes that you will join a religious organization. **198**
To see others shaking a tambourine, is a sign of approaching marriage. **030**

TAPE MEASURE—To see one in your sleep, denotes that you will be justified in conducting a certain affair. **125**
To use one, denotes an honest and comfortable life. **400**

TAPE WORM—This is an extremely good omen to policy players. **932**

TAPIOCA—To drink it denotes a happy extermination of differences among friends and relatives. **215**

TAR—To dream of tar, to a young woman, it denotes that she will marry a respectable dark man. **315**
To a man vice-versa. **357**

TASK MASTER—Denotes grief and vexation. It also denotes loss of health. **015**

TAVERN—To visit one denotes excessive pleasure accompanied by a great deal of smoking and drinking. **269**

TAXICAB—To drive one, denotes loss of valuable time. **569**
To see others driving a taxicab, denotes an unprofitable investment. **676**

TEA—To drink tea, denotes great prudence and popularity. **161**

TEAPOT—To dream of a teapot, denotes a scandal **447**

By Prof. De Herbert 151

TEA ROOM—To visit one, denotes that you will associate with some of the finest families in the community in the near future. **138**

TEACHER—To dream of one denotes a successful and outstanding career. This is truly an excellent dream for all. **134**

TEACUP—To use one denotes joy and profit. **600**
To break one, denotes that your enemies are more than a match for you. **444**

TEAM—To dream of a team of horses, denote an excellent position; short hours and good pay. **335**

TEAM OF HORSES—To dream of a team of horses, signify much prosperity and good health. **433**

TEAR—To shed a tear, denotes joy and profit. **226**

TEAR BOMB—To dream of a tear bomb, denotes that your effort is in vain. Abandon the course, that you are now pursuing. **377**

TEAR GAS—Denotes destruction and lost hopes. This is a bad omen to all. **196**

TEASPOON—Denotes that it will be necessary to be treated by a doctor in order to regain your health. **116**

TEETH—To dream that your teeth drop out, denotes disappointment. **144**
To wear false teeth, denotes an unfaithful lover. **143**
To dream of pretty white teeth, denotes wealth and good health. **400**

TELEGRAM—To receive one, denotes prosperity and long life. **718**

TELEPHONE—To hear one ring, denotes joy. **918**

TELEPHONE OPERATOR—To talk to one, denotes that some one will give you a tip, on some important matter, which would place a great deal of money at your disposal. **572**
profit. It also denotes that you will receive a costly present from one of your sweethearts. **606**

TELESCOPE—To look through one, denotes that you will discover a startling secret. **390**

TENNIS—To play tennis, denotes gratified ambition. **432**

TENNIS COURT—To visit one denotes joy and much prosperity. It also indicates extraordinary good health. **216**

TENT—To dream of one denotes protection and good luck in all of your affairs. **552**

THANKSGIVING DAY—To dream of this celebrated day denotes joy and much happiness. **642**

THEATRE—To visit one, denotes that you will see an old friend, whom you have not seen for a great many years. **919**
    To see a crowded theatre, denotes that you will hear pleasant news. **517**

THERMOMETER—To see one in your sleep denotes good fortune on the following day. It also promises that your business will succeed. **200**

THERMOS BOTTLE—To dream of one, denotes a pleasant journey. **939**

THIEF—To dream of a thief, denotes vexation. **110**

THIMBLE—To use one, is a sign of comfort and a little prosperity. **127**

THIRSTY—Denotes want and suffering. **328**

THORNE—To dream of a thorne, denotes that you will be outwitted by your enemies. **156**

THRONE—To see a sovereign sitting upon a throne, denotes everlasting peace and prosperity. **137**
    To dream that you sit upon a throne, denotes an increase in salary. **341**

THUNDER—To dream of thunder, denotes sad news. **198**

TICKET—To purchase one denotes successful adventure. **215**

TICKLE—To dream that you are being tickled denotes sudden joy. **138**

TIDE—To dream of the tide is a sign of a loving partner. **111**

TIE PIN—Denotes gain and popularity. **255**

TIGER—To dream of one denotes a misunderstanding, which may lead to a fight. **563**

TIGER CAT—To dream of one, denotes a deadly enemy. **534**

TILTMAN—To see one in your sleep denotes that you will succeed in obtaining your wishes. **534**

TIMEKEEPER—Denotes an increase in knowledge as well as salary. **256**

TIMEPIECE—Denotes luxury and much happiness. **345**

TIP—To dream that you receive a tip, denotes a wasted life. **281**

TIRE—To dream of one, denotes a change of address for the better. **518**

TIRED—To be fatigued in your sleep denotes hardship for a while. **021**

TISSUE PAPER—To dream of tissue paper, denotes that you will solve a baffling mystery. **310**

TOBACCO—Denotes that the prisoner will obtain a speedy release. **671**

TOBACCO SHOP—To visit one denotes that your ship is coming in this week. **369**

TOENAILS—To dream of your toenails is a sign of deceit and treachery. Some one is greatly opposed to you. **291**

TOILET—To be in the toilet, denotes excessive pleasure. **547**

TOMATOES—To see ripe tomatoes, is a sign of approaching prosperity. **326**
Young tomatoes denote great anxiety and persecution. **566**

TOMB STONE—Denotes the loss of a dear friend or relative. **418**

TOOLS—To dream of using any kind of tools, denote business success. **121**

TOOTH ACHE—To dream of one denotes mischief. **706**

TOOTH BRUSH—Is a sign of misunderstanding among lovers. **315**

TORCH LIGHT—To see one in your sleep, denotes that you are religiously inclined. **316**

TORMENTED—To be tormented in your sleep is a sign of worries and disgust. **357**

TOURIST—To see a tourist denotes a family's jar. **182**
To dream that you are a tourist, denotes notoriety. **407**

TOWBOAT—To see one, in your sleep, denotes distress, and loss of ambition. **564**

TOWEL—A clean towel denotes joy and profit. **769**
An unclean towel denotes failure in business. **611**

TOWER—To dream of one is a sign that your liberty is threatened. **241**

TOWROPE—Denotes that you will have a poor chance in escaping from being drawn into a plot. **365**

TOY—To play with any kind of a toy, denotes that your friends are deceitful. Do not trust them any more. **394**

TRAIN—To see a moving train denotes a successful career. **441**
A still train, denotes honor. **518**

TRAITOR—To dream of one, is a sign of approaching danger. **372**

TRAMP—To see one, denotes that you will be insulted by an ignorant person. **576**

TRANSLATOR—To see one in your sleep, denotes that you will visit a foreign shore in years to come. **366**

TRAP—To see one, denotes that you will get a job where you can help yourself. Do not take too much at once. Let your conscience be your guide. 379

TRAVEL—To travel on horse back, denotes good luck and the picture of good health. 816

To travel on foot, signifies slow progress. 161

To travel on water denotes a profitable undertaking 760

To travel by air is a sign of glorification and success 291

TRAY—To carry one on your head, denotes ordinary circumstances, 641

To carry one in your hand is a sign of joy and happiness. 362

TREASURE—To discover a treasure, denotes that you will fall heir to an inheritance. 382

TREE—A green tree denotes sickness. 568

A dried tree, denotes loss of appetite. 409

TRIANGLE—To dream of one, denotes success. This is an excellent dream to those who invest in games of chances. 333

TROLLEY CAR—To ride on one, denotes that you will succeed in obtaining profitable employment not very far from your home. 316

TROMBONE—Denotes security in business, and success in love affairs. 792

TROUSERS—To dream of a torn trousers, is a sign of disappointment and vexation. 182

A pair of new trousers, is a sign of good luck on the following day. 419

TUB—Denotes domestic tranquility. 404

A tub of muddy water or unclean clothes, denotes that some one is trying to ruin your reputation. 615

TUBERCULOSIS—To dream of this disease, denotes that your health is declining. This dream warns you to consult a physician at once. 767

TUG OF WAR—Denotes mischief. 561

TUNNEL—To pass under a tunnel, denotes safety of your affairs. **616**

TURKEY—To see one, denotes prosperity and good fortune. **544**

TURPENTINE—Denotes sickness. **563**

TURTLE—To dream of one denotes a disease. **357**

TURTLEDOVE—To see one, denotes that you will receive a declaration of love from your sweetheart. This is an excellent dream to lovers. **386**

TUXEDO—To see a man dressed in a tuxedo, denotes that your sweetheart, has many lovers and admirers. **612**
To wear one yourself, denotes power and dignity. **569**

TWINS—If a woman dreams of having twins, it denotes that she will have a beautiful baby son soon. **221**

TWIST MOUTH—To see a twist mouth person, denotes that you are being scandled by your neighbors. They are jealous of your progress and indomitable courage. **841**

TYPEWRITER—Denotes that your business will grow larger and larger. Your progress is unlimited. **062**
To use one yourself is a sign of happiness. **210**

TYPIST—To a young girl, she will marry a prosperous young fellow. To a young man, he will marry a beautiful young girl. **679**

UGLY—To see an ugly person, denotes a successful career. **116**

UKULELE—To play one, denotes that you will become a great sportsman, as the years roll on. **603**

UMBRELLA—Denotes shelter to the poor and fatherless. To others it denotes security in business. **182**

UNCLE—To dream of your uncle, denotes success in business and in travels. **144**

UNCLE-IN-LAW—To dream of your uncle-in-law,

denotes quarrels. **667**

UNCONSCIOUS—To see an unconscious person, denotes that you will use very poor judgment in conducting a certain affair. **238**

UNCOVER—To uncover anything, denotes that you will obtain your wishes. **156**

UNDERCLOTHES—Silk underclothes is a sign of prosperity and good health. Cotton undergarment, denotes want and sufferings. **606**

UNDERTAKER—To see one, denotes that you will inherit a little wealth at the death of a relatives. **293**

To dream that you sit in an undertaker's parlor, denotes grief and vexation of spirit. **635**

UNDERWORLD—To come in contact with the underworld guys, denote that you will find yourself in a very embarrassing position. **521**

UNDRESS—To undress in the presence of others, denotes that you will form the acqaintance of a person of questionable character. **291**

To undress alone, in your room, denotes honesty and sincerity. **300**

UNFURNISHED ROOM—Denotes ordinary circumstances. **518**

UNLAWFUL ACT—To dream that you commit an unlawful act, denotes that you should avoid a certain person, who speaks unkind words in a sweet tone. **798**

UNLOCK—To unlock a door, denotes that there is one who loves you dearly. His love is as strong as death. **735**

UNLUCKY—To dream of being unlucky, denotes the reverse. You will be very lucky in the near future. **345**

UNMASK—To see a masked person unmasked, denotes that you will attend a prominent, social function. **319**

UNSADDLE—To unsaddle a horse, denotes a peaceful life. **263**

UNWELL—To dream of being unwell denotes joy and happiness. **419**

UPSPRING—To witness one, denotes persecution. **675**

UPSTAIRS—To go up stairs, denotes that you will become exceedingly rich by and by. It also indicates extraordinary good health, and enjoyment among friends and relatives. **454**

UTENSILS—Denote a happy reunion among friends and relatives. **983**

VACANT—To dream of visiting a vacant spot, denotes that there will be a notorious kidnaping in the village.. **632**

VACATION—To go on your vacation, denotes that you will hold a government position in the future. **537**

VACCINATE—To dream of vaccination, denotes a terrible disease is threatening the vicinity. **273**

VACUUM CLEANER—To use one, denotes that you will succeed in obtaining a position with a wealthy family. **236**

VAGABOND—To dream of one denotes that the prisoner will be exonorated. **221**

VALET—To dream of hiring a valet denotes power and dignity. **541**
If you are a valet, it denotes that you are of a quiet disposition and open character. It also indicates ordinary circumstances. **151**

VANITY BOX—To dream of one denotes that you are a self-centered person. **158**

VARNISH—To use it denotes that you will succeed in obtaining a beautiful set of furniture. **137**

VASELINE—To rub with it, denotes peace and satisfaction. **406**
To see others using it, denotes a loving wife or husband. **119**

VAUDEVILLE—Denotes joy and profit. It also denotes that your sweetheart means well towards you. **085**

VAULT—Denotes safety of your affairs. **405**

VEAL—If a young woman dreams of veal, it denotes that she will be delivered by a beautiful baby boy. **252**

VEGETABLE—To see a great deal of vegetables, denote peace and much prosperity. **645**

VENISON—Denotes that you will become a celebrated hunter and sportsman. **217**

VERDICT—To hear one, denotes that you will receive a shock. **151**

VESSEL—To see one sailing in fine weather denotes long life and prosperity. **316**
Bad weather denotes loss of health. **118**

VESTIBULE—To sit in your vestibule, denotes everlasting peace and prosperity. **291**
To sit in the vestibule of others, denotes a sorrowful life. **399**

VETERAN—To see one denotes safety of your affairs. It also promises honor. **116**

VIAL—To dream of a vial, denotes that some one is trying to poison you. But that person will never succeed because you do not associate with that party very much. **397**

VICHY WATER—To drink it at home, denotes prosperity. **567**
To drink it, in a public place, denotes courage. **303**

VICTORY—To win any kind of a victory, denotes long life and happiness. **600**

VICTROLA—To hear one play denotes pleasant news. **666**

VINEGAR—To drink it denotes mockery. **463**
To see others drink denotes that you will succeed in obtaining a loan. **495**

VIRGIN—To see one, denotes love and much happiness. It further denotes that you will be rewarded for your honorable conduct. **137**

VOLCANO—To dream of one, denotes that your effort is in vain at present. This dream warns you to change your method of procedure in dealing with a certain situation. **385**

VOLSTEAD ACT—To dream of the Volstead Act, denotes destruction and loss of ambition. **128**

VOMIT—To vomit denotes that you will cause much trouble to a dear friend, by talking a little too much. **653**

VOTE—To dream that you vote, denotes power and dignity. It also denotes, that you are greatly interested in the development and the welfare of the nation. **177**

VOUCH—To vouch for any one, denotes that you will form the acquaintance of one in power. **123**

VOW—To make a vow in your sleep, signifies that you will make and keep a solemn promise to a dying friend or relative. **362**

VOYAGE—To take a voyage, denotes that your hopes will materialize shortly. **275**

VULGAR—To dream of seeing anything vulgar, denotes shame and remorse. **226**

WAFFLES—Denotes peace and prosperity of long duration. **375**

WAGON—To dream of a filled wagon signifies business success. **541**
To dream of an empty wagon, denotes loss of appetite. **700**

WAGES—To dream that your wages have been reduced denotes discontent. An increase in salary, denotes peace and satisfaction. **940**

WAISTCOAT—To wear one, denotes that you will succeed in obtaining a decent position with a good salary. **359**

WAITER—To dream of a waiter, denotes an elevation in fortune. **932**
To dream that you are a waiter, signifies that you will join a patriotic organization. **516**

WALK—To dream of walking a long distance, signifies that you will encounter great difficulties in carrying your plans. Nevertheless, you wll finally succeed. **233**
To walk a short distance is a sign of ambiton. **041**

WALL—To see a large wall, denotes protection of your affairs. **773**

WALNUTS—Signify that your efforts will be rewarded financially. **562**

WALTZ—To see people waltz, is a sign of approaching marriage. **681**
To walz yourself, denotes everlasting peace and prosperity. **356**

WAR—To dream of war, denotes misery and disappointment. **166**

WARDEN—To see one denotes that one in whom you are interested will be confined in a hospital for a few weeks. **191**

WARDROBE—A filled wardrobe, signifies luxury; beautiful and expensive jewels and fine clothes. **167**
An empty wardrobe, is a sign of anxiety and dissatisfaction. **344**

WAREHOUSE—To visit one, denotes that you will pawn something of great value. **961**

WARNING—To receive a warning in your sleep, is a sure sign of precaution. Be careful in the manner in which you conduct your business at present. **777**

WARRANT—Denotes trouble and anxiety. **782**

WARRIOR—Denotes a powerful enemy. **023**

WARSHIP—To see one, in your sleep, denotes that

you will triumph over your enemies in every way. **160**

WART—To dream that your body is covered with warts denotes riches and good health. **935**

WASH—To wash clothes, denotes a peaceful mind. **699**

To wash yourself, denotes an honorable career. **532**

To wash others, is a sign of thrift. **381**

WASH BASIN—Denotes peace and satisfaction. **341**

WASHWOMAN—To see one in your sleep, denotes that you will rise above your present position, and be happy for the rest of your life. **676**

WASHSTAND—To visit one, denotes joy and profit. **393**

WASTE-BASKET—To see one, denotes that you will receive a letter; the contents of which you would not wish to hear. **127**

WATCH—Denotes that some one is tracing your conduct. **354**

WATCHMAN—Denotes that you will lose a part of your saving, by acting too hastily. "Everything that shines, is not gold." **537**

To fight with a watchman, denotes that you will succeed in gaining possession of a certain property. **378**

WATER—To dream of clear water, denotes health, wealth, and much happiness. **116**

Muddy or foul water denotes loss. **110**

WATER SPOUT—Denotes good health and prosperity. **065**

WATER WHEEL—Denotes sudden wealth accompanied by a host of sincere friends. **405**

WAVES—To see large waves denote family quarrels. **316**

Small waves, signify a peaceful mind. **593**

WAX—To use it, denotes that your friends will aid

you financially. **162**

WEAPON—Denotes danger from an unexpected source. **279**

WEDDING—To dream of a wedding, denotes a funeral, generally the death of a relative or a dear friend. **394**

WEDDING CAKE—To dream of one denotes a successful career. **101**

WEEDS—To dream that your garden or farm land is covered with weeds, denote that your neighbors are jealous of you. **211**

WEEKLY PAYMENT—Denotes that you are making a mistake by not taking hold of the proposition that is being offered to you. **100**

WEEP—To weep in your sleep is a sure sign of joy and prosperity. It signifies good luck in games of chances. **242**

WEIGH—To weigh yourself, denotes that your wife or husband has lost confidence in you. **183**

WELCOMING KISS—To be the receipient of one, denotes exaggerated pleasure. **347**

WELL DRESSED PERSON—To see a smartly dressed person in your sleep denotes long life and prosperity. **010**

WEST INDIAN—To dream of one, denotes success in all your undertakings. It is a sign of power and dignity accompanied by sudden wealth. It also denotes luxury. **737**

WHALE—To see one in your sleep denotes an abundance of wealth. **142**
To ride on the back of a whale denotes that you will succeed in obtaining your wishes. **241**

WHARF—To be at the wharf, denotes a pleasant journey. **694**

WHEAT—To dream of an abundance of wheat, is a sign of great prosperity. It is a sign of good crops to farmers. **573**

WHEEL—To dream of a wheel, denotes that you will succeed in obtaining the position that you desire. **265**

WHEELBARROW—To see one in your sleep, denotes that you will obtain a position, in which you will be obliged to stand on your feet a great deal. **525**

WHEELWRIGHT—Denotes ordinary circumstances. You will always be in a position to supply your daily need, but you will never be rich. **675**

WHIP—To dream of a whip denotes that you will triumph over your enemies. **769**

To dream that you are being whipped denotes disgrace. **600**

To dream of whipping someone, signifies power and dignity. **202**

WHIRLPOOL—Denotes a dangerous career. **262**

WHIRLWIND—Denotes secret sorrows. **430**

WHISKY—To drink it, denotes trouble and anxiety. **219**

To turn away from it, denotes peace and satisfaction. **291**

WHIST—To play whist denotes pleasure and good fortune. **243**

WHISTLE—To whistle in your sleep, denotes gratified ambition. It also indicates popularity. **221**

To hear others whistle, denotes a peaceful mind. **222**

WHITE DRESS—Denotes good luck in games of chances. **100**

WHITE MAN—To dream of one denotes loss of reputation. It also indicates law suits. **768**

WHITE WOMAN—Denotes business success. It also denotes courage and great ability. **798**

WHOOPING COUGH—Denotes that your friends are faithful. **073**

WIDOW—To see one, denotes that you will fall heir

to an estate. **369**

To talk to one, denotes that you will marry for money and not for love. **569**

WIFE—To dream of your wife denotes that she loves you dearly. It also indicates that she is doing all that is in her power to make you happy. **117**

WILDERNESS—Denotes business difficulties for a very short time. **333**

WILL—To dream of one denotes safety of your affairs. **428**

WIN—To dream that you win a prize or any kind of game, denotes great success. **367**

WIND MILL—To see a wind mill in operation, denotes a brilliant future. **191**

If the mill is standing still, it is a sign of slow progress. **193**

WINDOW—To be looking out at your window, denotes a loving wife or husband. It also denotes a peaceful mind. **396**

WINE—To drink it, denotes merriment, and much satisfaction. It denotes a prosperous life. **679**

WINE CELLAR—Denotes long life and happiness. **144**

WINE GLASS—Signifies great ambitions. **210**

WINGS—To dream that you have a pair of wings, denotes that one of your sons, will become a great aviator. **383**

WINTER—To dream of winter at another time of the year, denotes distress. **394**

WIRE—To dream of a wire, denotes that you will obtain your wish, by paying graft. **241**

WISDOM TOOTH—To dream of this particular tooth, denotes that you will be enlightened on a particular subject. **232**

WITCH—To dream of one, mark her words carefully, and follow her instructions to a certain extent.

Watch for your number. **236**

WITNESS—To dream that you are a witness in a case, denotes that there is some one, who wants to control your affairs. **133**

WIZARD—To dream of one, denotes that you will visit a fortune teller in order to be advised on a certain matter. **299**

WOLF—To dream of one denotes dangerous enemies in sheep's clothing. **387**

WOMAN—If a man dreams that he is a woman, it denotes a weak mind. **541**

If a woman dreams that she is a man, it denotes power and dignity. **427**

WONDERLAND—To be in wonderland, denotes strange experience. **215**

WOOD—To chop wood, denotes a hard winter. **732**

To see others chopping wood, denotes that your hope will be realized. **233**

WOOD ALCOHOL—To drink it, denotes sad news. It also indicates a dreary life. **143**

WORK—To dream that you are at work, denotes that your aim will be accomplished. **545**

WORKHOUSE—To be in one, denotes shame and misery. **214**

WORKSHOP—Denotes ordinary circumstances. **184**

WORM—Denotes good luck in games of chances. This is a sure sign of sudden wealth and prosperity. **932**

WORSHIP—To dream that you worship any one, denotes that you will rob a friend in the near future. **568**

WOUND—To dress a wound, denotes comfort and long life. It also denotes that you will become a nurse or a charitable worker. **761**

WRAPPING PAPER—Denotes great success in business. **232**

WRECK—To see a wreck, denotes lost hopes. **172**

WRESTLE—To wrestle with any one denotes ambition and power. **727**

WRIST WATCH—Denotes a pleasant sorprise. It also indicates much wealth. **025**

WRITING PAPER—Denotes that you will receive a letter whicn will contain good news. **345**

WRITE A LETTER—To write a letter, denotes that you will succeed in marrying the one whom you love. **111**

X-RAY—To have an X-ray of your body, denotes that one of your friends is a little indisposed, and needs your assistance. **364**

XYLOPHONE—Denotes success in love and travels. **328**

YACHT—To ride in one denotes joy and profit. **319** To own your own private yacht, signifies prosperity and much happiness. **942**

YACHTSMAN—To dream of a yachtsman, denotes that you will become a great sportsman in the near future. **444**

YAMS—To eat them denotes riches and much gaiety. **309**

YANKEE—To dream of one denotes that some one is trying to learn all about your affairs. **868**

YARD—Denotes wealth and happiness. **366** To see children playing in a backyard denotes long life and happiness. **360**

YARDSTICK—To measure with one, denotes thrift. **736**

YEAST—To dream of yeast, denotes that you will become stout in the near future. **934**

YELL—To yell in your sleep, denotes a troubled spirit. **568**

YELLOW—To dream of anything yellow, denotes suc cess in all of your undertakings. **336**

YELLOW FEVER—Denotes contentment. **768**

YOKE—To see one in your sleep, denotes a burdened mind.
121

YOUNG—To dream that you have grown younger denotes an elevation of fortune. **319**

YEW—To see a yew tree in your sleep denotes long life and prosperity. **215**

YUCCA—To dream of this tropical vegetable, denotes peace and satisfaction. **187**

YULETIDE—To dream of the yuletide, denotes prosperity. **369**

ZEBRA—To see one in your sleep, denotes wild thoughts. **226**

ZEPPELIN—Denotes an elevation of fortune. It also indicates a pleasant voyage. **421**

ZERO—To dream of zero, is a sign of discomfort. **001**

ZERO WEATHER—Denotes protection to the home-less and destitute. **038**

ZIGZAG—To dream of running zigzag, denotes that you will barely escape from being drawn into a plot.
157

ZINK—To dream of zink, denotes shelter and protection to the homeless. **144**

ZIP—To carry one, denotes that you will have an enjoyable time among friends. **639**

ZODIAC—To dream of the zodiac signs, denotes a successful career. Your life will be filled with sunshine and you will live happily at all times. **736**

ZOOLOGICAL GARDEN—To visit one, denotes that you will gain a great deal of experience from your present transactions. **763**

ZULU—To dream of one denotes success in all of your adventures. It also promises long life and security. **302**

LETTERS

A — 387		N — 407	
B — 532		O — 293	
C — 765		P — 561	
D — 183		Q — 532	
E — 196		R — 161	
F — 426		S — 587	
G — 319		T — 421	
H — 528		U — 217	
I — 217		V — 411	
J — 584		W — 514	
K — 576		X — 589	
L — 184		Y — 716	
M — 217		Z — 428	

THE DAYS OF THE WEEK

Monday	761	Friday	392
Tuesday	281	Saturday	769
Wednesday	133		
Thursday	287	Sunday	284

THE MONTHS OF THE YEAR

January	183	July	118
February	576	August	196
March	234	September	108
April	771	October	282
May	291	November	285
June	567	December	033

NAMES

LADIES' LIST (With Their Symbols)

ABIGAIL—Symbolizes love, virtue and sincere friendship. It also indicates an inclination for the finer things of life. **194**

ADA—Signifies truth, honesty and good will toward all. It is truly the symbol of affection. **253**

ADIA—Indicates the sweetness of the morning glory and the pride of one's heart. It stands for the joy and essence of life. **425**

ADELINE—Symbolizes greatness and achievements of the highest degree. It is a name of fame and wealth. **677**

AIMEE—Signifies high endeavour and good understanding. It also signifies long life. **121**

AGNES—Is the spirit of high esteem. Love, joy and jollity are some of the essential traits. **124**

ALBERTHA—Signifies power, wealth and a very successful career. This is truly an excellent name. **283**

ALICE—Symbolizes gaiety, love, and a successful marriage. It also indicates an ambitious and active life. **485**

ALEXANDRIA—Signifies beauty enriched with all the necessities of life, surrounded by pomp and valor. **144**

ALLIE—Denotes the love of education and the uplifting of humanity. **306**

ALMA—Signifies the rose of Sharon and the lily of the valley. It stands for everything that is charming and fascinating. **220**

AMELIA—Symbolizes daring and adventure, accompanied by great deal of wealth and popularity. **765**

AMABEL—Signifies profound thought intermingled

with gaiety and other luxurious pleasures and entertainments. It also denotes honesty. **235**

AMBER—Signifies long life and a successful career. **171**

ANETTE—Portrays a sweet, loving disposition. It also indicates a successful marriage. **196**

ANNIE—Signifies the break of hearts. It indicates a charming and bewitching personality. Many admirers but only one will be accepted. **331**

ANTONIA—Signifies gratified ambition, also good health and great friendship. **163**

ANNA—Personifies sweetness, bashfulness and greatness. It also denotes firm integrity and ardent love. **105**

ANGELINE—Is the essence of sweetness and charming personality. Courtship is one of the outstanding characteristics of this name. **773**

ARDELINE—Symbolizes the charm and joys of life, accompanied by all traditions of the lovers. It clearly indicates romance in abundance. **216**

ARABELLA—Signifies long life and prosperity. It also indicates that love is inevitable. This name signifies pleasant personality and the ability to gain a host of friends. **145**

AUGUSTA—Symbolizes good fortune, and a successful marriage, surrounded by amiable friends and relatives. **717**

AURELIA—Signifies pleasant surprises and a love for travel and adventure. **163**

AURORA—Denotes a loving husband and many beautiful and lovable children. **142**

BEATRICE—Symbolizes honesty and culture. It also indicates an abundance of fascinating lovers. **173**

BEATRIX—Signifies wealth, and the picture of good health. **173**

BERTHA—Symbolizes beauty and charm. It also indicates a loving disposition and charming personality. **965**

BERYL—Is the baby face darling, so gentle and yet so sweet. This name indicates true virtue. **453**

BERNICE—Symbolizes a pleasant and charming life, filled with gaiety. It also indicates popularity among the opposite sex. **276**

BESSIE—Symbolizes truth and honesty. Marriage is generally a success. **376**

BETSY—Denotes love and affection to a remarkable degree. **425**

BEULAH—Signifies heroism and aptitude for the better things of life. **711**

BRIDGET—Symbolizes faith in one's self. Success is generally attained. **376**

CATHERINE—Is the sweetheart of all ages. It indicates faithfulness and sincerity in love affairs. **783**

CAMILLA—Symbolizes the morning glory, and the lily of the valley, sweet as sweet can be, charming to the eyes, and joy to one's heart and affection. **259**

CAESAR—Denotes gallantry and admiration. **657**

CASSANDRA—Symbolizes love and jealousy, but very affectionate. **306**

CECILIA—Represents power and dignity accompanied by great wealth. **229**

CHARLOTTE—Symbolizes uprightness in all transactions. It stands for purity and affection. **446**

CHARITY—Signifies a life of happiness and self-reliance. **122**

CHRISTIANA—Is the symbol of kind affection, and strong love affairs. Peace and satisfaction are ever present. **316**

CHLOE—Is the symbol of long life and satisfaction. **716**

CICELY—Denotes wealth in abundance, accompanied by a gay life. 167

CLARISO—Is a symbol of good nature and self-reliance with love as a dominating factor. 123

CLEOPATRA—Is the darling lover of all ages. 283

CLEMENTINE—Signifies ambition and reliability. It also represents the brightness of the morning star. 315

CORA—Symbolizes love and content, and unlimited devotion. 405

CORDELLA—Signifies beautfy, and sincere friendship. 341

CORINA—Symbolizes the beautiful flower, that one finds deep in the forest with all its fragrance and charm. 213

CORNELIA—Signifies the spirit of adventure and success. 162

CONSTANCE—Is the symbol of a successful career, accompanied by extraordinary good health. 145

CYNTHIA—Symbolizes love and affection. 213

DAUGHERTY—Is the symbol of power and dignity. 176

DEBORAH—Symbolizes the love of created art, and a passion for the finer things of life. 506

DELIA—Is the symbol of long life and prosperity. 213

DELLIE—Indicates loveliness, kindness, and good will toward all mankind. 118

DIANA—Symbolizes greatness and sincerity of all ages. 216

DORIS—Symbolizes greatness and gratified ambition; always reaching for the best things in life. 727

DORINE—Is the personification of gaiety and much admiration. 414

DOROTHEA—Symbolizes love, and the milk of human kindness. 283

DOROTHY—Represents the joys of life and the glorious conception of universal festivity and social enjoyment. **182**

EDITH—Is the symbol of intelligence and good fortune. **344**

EDNA—Is the symbol of loveliness. Keep sweet as you are Edna. **253**

ELAINE—Is the symbol of purity. Elaine the beautiful; Elaine the wonderful; Elaine the lily maid of Astolat. **893**

ELENA—Symbolizes beauty and success in love affairs. **17**

ELLA—Signifies glorified ambition and a successful career. **335**

ELLEN—Symbolizes purity and love for the finer things of life. **718**

ELEANOR—Is the symbol of loveliness, also, sweet and loveable. **223**

ELLIE—is the symbol of admiration. It also indicates long life and security. **163**

ELIZA—Symbolizes firm integrity, and good understanding. **165**

ELIZABETH—Symbolizes honor and greatness. It also indicates power and dignity. **231**

ELVIRA—Symbolizes the morning glory, and the sweet budding flower. **173**

EMELINE—Symbolizes sweetness, and a life of endearment. **516**

EMMA—Symbolizes popularity among friends and relatives. **233**

ENID—Is the symbol of joy and jollity. It also indicates a desire for beautiful things. **716**

ERMAINE—Stands for purity, and sincerity. **143**

ERMINE—Is the symbol of unlimited devotion and self-sacrifice in behalfs of humanity. **286**

ERNESTINE—Is the symbol of love and devotion. **607**

ESSIE—Symbolizes great ambition in the business world. **173**

ESTELLE—Symbolizes virtue and piety. **534**

ESTHER—Symbolizes the joy of one's heart and kind affection. **534**

ETHEL—Is the symbol of great friendship, and the uplifting of the human race. **156**

ETHELIND—Is the symbol of progress, and firm devotion. **156**

ETTA—Symbolizes the love of religion. It also indicates the love for beautiful things and admiration. **384**

EUNICE—Symbolizes the brightness of the morning star, and the noonday sun. **234**

EURICE—Is the symbol of loveliness, and the love for the arts and the sciences. **219**

EVANGELINE—Is the symbol of love and the essence of sweetness. **937**

EVANGELINA—Symbolizes everlasting devotion, and firm integrity. **937**

EVE—Symbolizes happiness and unlimited friendship. **194**

EVELINE—Is the symbol of peaceful existence. **216**

FANNIE—Is the symbol of long life and prosperity. **675**

FAUSTINA—Is the symbol of loveliness, accompanied by a host of true friends. **326**

FREDRECIA—Symbolizes harmony and great success in all transactions. **165**

FIDELA—Is the symbol of peace and satisfaction. **132**

FLORA—Denotes a charming life, filled with sunshine and great devotion. **367**

FLOY—Is the symbol of charm and delight. **421**

FLORY—Symbolizes the eye for beautiful things and serene surrounding. **213**

FRANCIS—Symbolizes loyalty and kindness, tender and loving. **506**

GEORGIE—Symbolizes ambition and good fortune, always reaching out for better things. **334**

GERTRUDE—Is the symbol of love and fortune. **204**

GEORGIANE—Is the symbol of happiness and extraordinary good health accompanied by great wealth. **617**

GERALDINE—Is a symbol of gaiety and much happiness. It also stands out for good health. **233**

GENEITHA—Symbolizes the display of pomp and valor. It indicates elaborate parties and high class association. **421**

GINA—Is a symbol of a bright future and a successful marriage. **183**

GLORIA—Is the symbol of devotion and a successful and outstanding career. **216**

GWENDOLYN—Is the symbol of glorified ambition. **273**

HADDIE—Indicates the joy maker and the life of the party. **195**

HAGAR—Indicates a glorious marriage. **671**

HANNAH—Symbolizes much happiness and marked prosperity. **364**

HARRIET—Is the symbol of a fantastic life with a great deal of variation. **176**

HAZEL—Is the symbol of long life and prosperity throughout the span of life. **534**

HELEN—Symbolizes purity and long life. **284**

HELENA—Is the symbol of everlasting friendship and a guiding star to the unfortunate. **557**

HENRIETTA—Symbolizes long life and much prosperity. **483**

HILDA—Symbolizes the joys of one's heart. **534**

HILARIA—Is the symbol of a happy and prosperous

Marriage. **613**

HORTENSE—Is the darling sweetheart of all ages. It is also the symbol of good fortune. **167**

IDA—Is the symbol of high esteem and a great desire for the best things of life. **657**

ILENE—Is the symbol of love for the arts and the sciences. It indicates keen judgment in general. **429**

INEZ—Symbolizes faith and stability. **117**

IONA—Is a symbol of a happy and a prosperous life. **596**

IOTA—Stands out for justice towards all men. It also represents the propensity for beautiful things. **294**

IRENE—Is the symbol of gaiety and splendor. **425**

IRIS—Personifies sincerity and undying devotion. **731**

ISABELLA—Symbolizes prominence and a fruitful life. **391**

ISILING—Is a symbol of splendor and loveliness. **167**

IVY—Symbolizes joy and jollity. It also indicates an abundance of life. **425**

JACQUELINE—Stands out for extraordinary good qualities, simple and lovable disposition. **661**

JANE—Is the darling of one's affection. **384**

JANET—Symbolizes faith and purity. **183**

JANIE—Symbolizes prominence and good fortune. **324**

JENNY—Is the symbol of long life and much happiness. **215**

JESSIE—Stands out for fame and fortune. **195**

JOANA—Is the symbol of much happiness. It also is a symbol of true friendship, and peace with the world. **018**

JOSEPHINE—Is the symbol of joy and prosperity. It also indicates a successful marriage. **661**

JOYCE—Symbolizes beauty and purity. **101**

JULIA—Is the symbol of long life and much

happiness. **716**

JULIET—Symbolizes the beauty and charm of womanhood. **297**

KATE—Is the symbol of magnificient splendor and a life of ease. **184**

KATHLEEN—Symbolizes the charms and the niceties of life. **323**

KATHERINE—Symbolizes the brightness of the noon-day sun and the evening star. **345**

KATY—Is the symbol of virtue. **123**

KETURAH—Is the symbol of everlasting joy and felicity. **723**

KEZIAH—Symbolizes peace and prosperity, also love and tenderness for those in distress. **133**

KEZIE—Stands out for truth and sincerity. **425**

KITTY—Is the symbol of fair play. **193**

LAURA—Symbolizes celestial charm and pleasant personality. This name represents beauty in every respect.

LOUISA—Symbolizes great happiness. **213**

LOUISE—Symbolizes virtue, loveliness, kindness and progress. **371**

LEE—Symbolizes high mindedness, yet very lovable. **111**

LENA—Symbolizes virtue, she also takes the part of the heroine. **949**

LENORA—Symbolizes piety and truthfulness; so gentle and yet so free with every one. Her charming smiles are always present. **194**

LEOTA—Symbolizes loveliness. She is the darling sweetheart of all ages. She is indeed the beloved of the universe. **419**

LETTIE—Symbolizes bravery and self deniance in the behalfs of mankind. **321**

LEWGEAN—Symbolizes love, virtue and sincerity. **215**

LILIA—Personifies the progressive and industrial person with a propensity to succeed in life. 879

LILLIAN—Is the symbol of peace and satisfaction. 287

LILA—Symbolizes true friendship and firm integrity. 687

LINA—Symbolizes love for the finer things of life. 495

LIZZY—Symbolizes perpetual happiness and firm devotion. 763

LORRAINE—Is the symbol of glory and jollification. 673

LOTTIE—Symbolizes self-abnegation. She is truly the spirit of admiration. 173

LUCILLE—Symbolizes great ambition. 394

LUCRETIA—Stands out for loyalty and gracefulness. 716

LUCY—Symbolizes the pure in heart. She is admired by people in all walks of life. 224

MABEI—Symbolizes the love for universal festivity and social enjoyment. 765

MABLE—Is the symbol of joy and much gaiety. 425

MAGDALINE—Symbolizes virtue and loveliness. 377

MAGGIE—Stands out for perpetual happiness. 234

MARJORIE—Symbolizes love, virtue and true friendship. 277

MALLY—Is the symbol of beauty and loveliness. 456

MAMMIE—Is the symbol of piety and devotion, always looking to go higher and higher to conquer the problems of life. 763

MAMES—Is the symbol of truth and sagacity. 742

MAMZETT—Is the symbol of power and dignity. 281

MARCELLA—Symbolizes eloquence and achievement. 192

MARGARET—Personifies the pure in heart, malice towards none and a word of good cheer for all. 273

MARGY—Symbolizes adoration and loveliness. Beauty to the eyes and to one's affection. **365**

MARGERY—Is the symbol of loyalty and graciousness. **224**

MARIA—Is the symbol of charm, beauty and sociability. This name stands out for everything that is sweet and genuine. **653**

MARION—Personifies the charming and the delightful lassie with a pleasant personality and good will towards all. **566**

MARIANNE—Is so gentle and true. She stands for divine love. **213**

MARTHA—Stands out for indomitable courage and self-perseverance in all undertakings. **437**

MAY—Symbolizes the charms and the loveliness of one's affecton, loving all and hating none. **281**

MAYBELL—Symbolizes the real lady with all the virtues of womanhood **567**

MATTIE—Stands for high ideals and undying devotion. **329**

MAUD—Symbolizes love and truth. **325**

META—Symbolizes the talented and the desire for the fine arts. **325**

MERCY—Is the symbol of innocence. **167**

MIGNON—Symbolizes bravery. **225**

MILDRED—Stands out for piety and obedience. **583**

MILLICENT—Symbolizes love and courage to succeed and overcome all difficulties in life. **219**

MINETO—Symbolizes great ambition for music and the other fine arts. **653**

MINERVA—Symbolizes the beautiful little flower by the wayside. **516**

MIRIANDO—Is the symbol of content and happiness. **163**

NANCY—Stands out for gaiety and a successful life. **567**

NAOMI—Symbolizes loyalty and loveliness. 016

NELL—Symbolizes the sweet and charming personality with the ever present smiles. 143

NETTIE—Symbolizes the dew that gently drops from heaven. 506

NICOLA—Stands out for an abundance of life. 134

NICIE—Symbolizes the true and the courageous. 386

NORENO—Symbolizes the fortunate girl, crowned with success and glory. 234

NORA—Symbolizes the beautiful and affectionate girl, filled with pity and compassion for the unfortunate. 193

ODESSA—Is the symbol of the lovable and adorable person. 393

OLIVIA—Symbolizes the glory of womanhood. 652

OLYMPHIA—Symbolizes a proud and dignified personality. 196

OPHELIA—Personifies the bold and striking physiology of womanhood. 275

ORA—Symbolizes a lovable and charming characteristic of divine devotion. 163

ORRIE—Stands out for fair play and good will towards all. 465

PATSEY—Symbolizes the lion-hearted and the lovable. 221

PATIENCE—Symbolizes the plain, simple, lovable person with a pleasant disposition and an unquestionable character. 763

PAULINE—Personifies the quiet and charming girl—so gentle and sweet. 283

PHILLIPA—Stands out for high endeavor, reaching out to attain the best things in life. 145

PHILLIS—Personifies the charitable and progressive intuition. 673

PHEBE—Symbolizes the ambitious and self controlled person. 136

PEARL—Is the personification of cleverness and a life devoted to the uplifting of the human race. **965**

PEGGY—Stands out for greatness and superiority. **233**

PINKY—Is the symbol of kindness and content. **612**

POLLY—Symbolizes the faithful and the courageous. **284**

PRUDENCE—Symbolizes the contented and the beloved person. **376**

RACHEL—Symbolizes the holy person, blessed by the almighty, and guided by his holy spirit. **959**

RAE—Symbolizes the courageous and the prudent. **384**

REBA—Personifies the upright and the out spoken character. **269**

REBECCA—Is the symbol of love and true devotion. **324**

REENIE—Personifies loveliness and charm. **126**

RHODA—Symbolizes the high minded and the prudent. **763**

ROSE—Is the symbol of the progressive the conscientious and the beloved lass. **283**

ROSIE—Personifies the dignified and the loveable. **321**

ROSALYN—Symbolizes the sweet little girl with the charming personality that lingers on through the ages. **194**

ROSAMIND—Stands out for piety and loveliness. **354**

RUBY—Symbolizes peace unity and concord. **671**

RUTH—Stands out for truth and unlimited courage. **126**

SABINA—Personifies the true and the faithful. **176**

SADIE—Personifies greatness and superiority. **287**

SALOME—Symbolizes the intelligent and the fearless. **381**

SALLY—Is the symbol of beauty and charm. **293**

SAPHIRA—Symbolizes the affectionate. **344**

SARAH—Symbolizes love and happiness. **293**

SIBYLLA—Symbolizes high endeavor to go forward

and conquer the problems of life. **516**

SELINA—Stands for great success. **135**

SHIRLEY—Stands out for high endeavour and material success. **184**

SUSANNAH—Symbolizes great futurity and long life. **623**

SYLVIA—Symbolizes the ambitious and the successful girl. It also stands for wisdom and the love of learning. **336**

TAMAR—Is the symbol of greatness and truth. **566**

THELIA—Personifies the honorable and the true lover. **426**

THEODORA—Symbolizes the sweet and the loveable. **367**

THEREST—Symbolizes sweetness and greatness. **224**

USALA—Symbolizes the darling sweetheart of all ages. **395**

URSEILA—Personifies the charming and the lovable. **213**

VALERIA—Personifies the true and the faithful. **103**

VALRICA—Stands for gaiety and splendor. **203**

VANITO—Personifies the intelligent and the faithful **456**

VIOLA—Is the symbol of high endeavour with a perspective view of reaching the great heights of fame and admiration. **173**

VIOLET—Is the symbol of kindness and lovable disposition, with tenderness and endearment for all. **400**

VIVIAN—Stands for long life and prosperity. A life of gaiety and much happiness. **284**

VICTORIA—Symbolizes the loveable and the true, with unlimited devotion and a pleasant personality. **761**

VIRGINIA—Is the symbol of ambition and success. **281**

WINNIE—Signifies love and kindness. **769**

WINNIFRED—Personifies the noble and the true. 221

WILHELMINA—Personifies honesty and truth. 514

WREN—Is the symbol of faithfulness and love. 223

WRENZO—Personifies the sweet and the lovable; charming in every respect; so gentle and yet so free. 576

ZENO—Symbolizes the peace maker. 114

ZENOLA—Is the symbol of intelligence and harmony. 767

GENTLEMEN'S LIST (With Their Symbols)

ABEL—Symbolizes the beloved and the contented. 134

ABRAHAM—Stands for courage, faithfulness and dominance. A true leader of the human race. 219

ABIATHER—Symbolizes the jolly fellow, filled with vim, vigor and vitality. 234

ABONIRAM—Personifies the man of iron and steel, strong personality and self reliance. 193

ADAM—Personifies the father and leader of the human race. 513

ALBERT—Represents the princely type—the ruler of men. 281

ALFONSO—Symbolizes the man of courage and responsibility. 194

ALLAN—Stands out for high ideals with a comprehensive understanding of life in general. 126

ALFRED—Symbolizes greatness and eloquence. 412

ALEXANDER—Symbolizes the happy warrior, dominating over the entire world, including man and beast. 213

ALONZA—Indicates the peaceful God-fearing man, working in unity with creation. 415

ALVIN—Is the symbol of will power and prominence. 216

ARMA—Indicates the healthy and the wealthy man. 194

AMOS—Personifies the celebrity, always in the spotlight. **226**

ANDREW—Stands for high endeavour and good will. **145**

ANGELO—Personifies peace and satisfaction. **221**

ANTHONY—Personifies shrewdness and oratory persuasion. **534**

ARMOND—Symbolizes the peaceful and kindly squire. **231**

ARCHIE—Stands out for steadfastness of purpose in order to conquer the problems of life. **193**

ARCHIBALD—Symbolizes progress. **443**

ARNOLD—Indicates smartness. **711**

ARON—Personifies the God-fearing man. **321**

ARTENAS—Stands for love, honor and high ideals. **217**

ARTHUR—Stands out for indomitable courage and precision. **416**

ASAHEL—Symbolizes the conscientious and the prudent man. **156**

AUBREY—Symbolizes the true and the faithful lover. **152**

AUGUSTINE—Symbolizes the leader of the race. **196**

AUSTIN—Symbolizes the successful industrialist. **234**

BAPTIST—Symbolizes the true sportsman and financier. **394**

BASIL—Represents the energetic and the emotional person. **126**

BEDFORD—Symbolizes the man of fortune and sociability. **233**

BARNABAS—Personifies the brilliant minded and the courageous. **121**

BARTHOLOMEW—Personifies the peaceful and the lovable character. **421**

BELLFIELD—Symbolizes the successful and the energetic business man. **113**

BENNETT—Personifies the hopeful and the beloved man. **192**

BENNIE—Symbolizes the playboy and the popular man. **412**

BENSON—Characterizes the rich and the benefactor. **617**

BENJAMIN—Represents God's chosen. **253**

BERISFORD—Symbolizes the oratory and skilful person. **162**

BERNARD—Personifies the proud and intelligent character. **142**

BERT—Personifies the successful and the intellectual. **941**

BERTRAM—Represents the valiant and the strong. It also indicate popularity among friends and relatives. **344**

BILL—Symbolizes the mamma's boy—spoiled by the motherly love and affection. **161**

BOBBY—Is the symbol of great attainments crowned with glory. **283**

BRANSON—Symbolizes a glamorous career. **102**

BULLY—Is the symbol of the fearless. **417**

BUNNIE—Characterizes an energetic and useful life, filled with vigor and vitality. **224**

BUSTER—Symbolizes power, dignity and grateful ambition. **101**

BYRON—Characterizes the pious and the energetic person. **164**

CAIN—Symbolizes the contented regardless of condition. **194**

CALDWELL—Symbolizes the leader of society. **162**

CALEB—Characterizes a sweet lovable disposition and generosity. **405**

CARROLL—Personifies the love of the arts and the sciences. It also indicates a successful and useful career. **617**

CEPHAS—Indicates long life and prosperity. **676**

CLAUDIUS—Personifies great intelligence and much learning.

CLIVE—Characterizes the man in high governmental position. **324**

CLEMENT—Stands out for wealth and happiness. **144**

CHARLES—Stands for indomitable courage and sagacity. **162**

CHRISTIAN—Personifies the religious person, tender and loving, with a good disposition. **162**

CHRISTOPHER—Represents the successful adventurer. **163**

CLIFFORD—Personifies the healthy, wealthy and wise **287**

CLARENCE—Characterizes the high-minded and self-reliance person. **163**

COLE—Stands out for keen judgment and cleverness. **215**

COLVIN—Characterizes true friendship and loyalty. **192**

CONRAD—Personifies the honest, progressive person, who is generally highly intellectual. **555**

CONSTANTINE—Symbolizes power and dignity. **156**

COSSIE—Stands out for sincerity and unlimited devotion. **227**

CRUGER—Stands for gallantry and power. **435**

CUTHBERT—Personifies the conservative person, very careful in all transactions. **211**

CYRUS—Stands out for great achievements in industry. **221**

DACOSTA—Stands for courage and power. **141**

DALRIMPLE—Symbolizes keen judgment and much prosperity. **253**

DAN—Personifies a man of the day. **211**

DANNIE—Symbolizes long life and prosperity. **376**

DANIEL—Personifies the God fearing man—prosperous and happy. **316**

DARIUS—Personifies the peaceful loving man. **506**

DELANO—Personifies will power and firm integrity. It also indicates courage of one's conviction. **412**

DAVID—Symbolizes God's annointed and a man after God's own heart. **911**

DEIGHTON—Symbolizes strength, good health and a lovable disposition. **165**

DEMETRIUS—Stands for high endeavour and achievements in the classical world. **283**

DICK—Represents the hghly intellectual and the progressive person. **519**

DONALD—Is noted for bravery dominance and skill. **912**

DONNELLY—Symbolizes the hero of modern times. **323**

DUDLEY—Symbolizes the conservative man. **225**

DUKE—Personifies the lover of music and the other fine arts. It also indicates wit, and a pleasant personality. **335**

DUNCAN—Indicates a kind and tender nature, noble and true in every respect. **765**

EARL—Personifies dignity and splendor. **765**

EBENEZER—Symbolizes social position and much wealth. **182**

EDGAR—Personifies great ability and self-reliance. **276**

ED—Symbolizes the beloved person, filled with love and tenderness for every one. **139**

EDDIE—Represents the true character. **152**

EDWARD—Personifies the successful industrialist. **723**

EGBERT—Symbolizes the author of extraordinary sagacity. **321**

ELDRED—Signifies the successful business man of keen intellect and sound judgment. **111**

ELI—Stands out for courage and fair play. 171

ELIZAH—Personifies the gifted and the pious man. 143

ELISHA—Symbolizes the man of great learning. 177

ELLIOTT—Personifies the creator of fashion and a lover of the arts. 223

ELDRED—Stands out for love and adventure. 916

ELMER—Indicates the creator of imaginary things. This is truly the inventive type. 328

EMANUEL—Stands for an amicable disposition and keen judgment. 213

ENOCH—Represents the peacemaker. 165

ERIC—Personifies the gentleman of leisure and great wealth. 107

ESAU—Represents the man of power and dignity. 193

ETHELDRED—Indicates the plain, simple lovable person with a tender heart and good will toward all. 152

EUGENE—Represents the mechanical genius. 152

EUSTACE—Symbolizes the smart fellow—very cunning. 142

EVERARD—Personifies the man of unlimited prospects and good fortune. 213

EZEKIEL—Personifies the God fearing man. 175

EZRA—Symbolizes the man of great intelligence and an able politician. 213

FELIX—Personifies the man of social ambition. 216

FERDINAND—Symbolizes the charming lover and the great hero of modern times. 314

FOREST—Personifies the man with a desire for wealth and power. 711

FRANK—Symbolizes the ambitious and the beloved man with a kindly disposition. 273

FRED—Personifies the man of good fortune and a kind heart, always willing to help those in distress. 576

GABRIEL—Personifies the kindly and good natured person. **201**

GAREY—Symbolizes the self-made man—the man with indomitable courage and perseverance. **305**

GERSHOM—Stands for loyalty and bravery. **283**

GERALD—Represents the kind and sympathetic person, with true love for his fellow men. **163**

GEORGE—Symbolizes the man of power and dignity, accompanied by riches in ab.:ndance. **273**

GIDEON—Personifies a man of a very few words, but a great scholar. **223**

GILBERT—Symbolizes the man with great ability, and a brilliant future. **163**

GLADSTONE—Personifies the man of extraordinary judgment of human frailty. It also symbolizes power and dignity. **883**

GODFREY—Symbolizes the ambitious and the industrious man. **113**

GOTTLIEB—Personifies honor and dignity. It also represents good fortune. **225**

GRAY—Stands out for good fortune and the picture of good health. **736**

GREGORY—Depicts greatness and power. **184**

HAMILTON—Symbolizes mechanical achievements. **739**

HAPPY—Represents the kind hearted fellow. **132**

HAROLD—Symbolizes the industrialist. It also indicates a great deal of prosperity and good health. **375**

HARRY—Symbolizes the ambitious man with a desire for advancement. **375**

HECTOR—Personifies the happy warrior, never bending to defeat. **213**

HENRY—Personifies the kingly type—a man of power and self-reliance. **161**

HORACE—Symbolizes the highly intellectual and the

well educated person. **213**

HERBERT—Personifies the man of power and dignity. It also indicates extraordinary executive ability which is the direct result of a successful and a prosperous career. **102**

HERMAN—Personifies good fortune and good health. **911**

HILTON—Symbolizes rare ability in commerce. **235**

HILARY—Represents the true and beloved sportsman. **193**

HORATIO—Personifies the kindly affectionate person of fortune. **325**

HOWARD—Symbolizes indomitable perseverance in spite of obstacles. He looks on the optimistic side of life. **634**

HUBERT—Personifies the happy go lucky fellow. **176**

HUGH—Symbolizes the propensity of elevation. **221**

HUMPHREY—Personifies the soldier of fortune and distinguished sportsman. **126**

ICHABOLD—Symbolizes the man of faith and good will. **143**

INGRAM—Personifies the prosperous business man. **194**

INNISS—Symbolizes the successful and the courageous warrior who never stops until the ultimate goal is attained. **234**

IRVINE—Personifies the jolly fellow. **562**

IRVINGTON—Symbolizes the aristocracy and the upright easy going person. **243**

ISAAC—Personifies the man of wealth and power. **911**

ISAIAH—Personifies the man of esteem, valor and prudence. **315**

ISRAEL—Symbolizes the true Christian. **227**

ISHMAEL—Stands for high endeavour and courage to conquer the problems of life. **216**

IVAN—Symbolizes the sturdy and the brilliant minded

man, with strength and determination to succeed in life. **216**

JACK—Symbolizes the traveler and the adventurer, who is beloved from pole to pole. **421**

JACKIE—Personifies the romantic type. **196**

JACOB—Symbolizes the great and prosperous leader of men. **293**

JARIUS—Symbolizes the man of natural born ability, to succeed in all undertakings, regardless of conditions. **324**

JAMES—Personifies the cave man of modern times. **535**

JEFF—Stands out for courage and self control. **425**

JERRY—Represents the tender loving warrior of human rights. **234**

JEROME—Symbolizes the fundamentalist, loyal and true to tradition. **155**

JIMMY—Personifies the happy and prosperous man, with a host of friends and relatives at his command. **194**

JOHN—Personifies the prosperous and intelligent business man. **216**

JONATHAN—Stands out for rightousness. **101**

JOSE—Personifies the ambitious man, with a propensity to dominate any situaton that may present itself. **617**

JOSEPH—Personifies the tender and loving man with a brilliant future. **215**

JOSHUA—Personifies the born and intellectual leader. It also stands out for brilliance and success. **394**

JOSIE—Represents the successful prospector. **615**

JOSIAH—Symbolizes the industrious and progressive person. **243**

JUDAH—Symbolizes the true arbitrator of human rights. **236**

JUDAS—Personifies the money changer. **194**

JUSTUS—Symbolizes the highly intelligent person, well versed in the history of the world, and that of human weakness. **717**

JULIUS—Personifies the successful warrior and the progressive business man. **224**

KARL—Personifies the sympathetic and good natured man, filled with the milk of human kindness. **233**

KELBY—Is truly the personification of wisdom accompanied by an outstanding career. **796**

KENDALL—Personifies the smart fellow. **183**

KENNETH—Represents the intellectual, the cultural and the successful business man. **121**

KENNEDY—Personifies the immortal hero of modern times. **326**

LABAN—Stands out for loyalty, courage and high endeavour. **326**

LAMBERT—Personifies the able mathematician and lecturer; well versed in this particular line. **223**

LANCELOT—Personifies gallantry to a remarkable degree. It also stands out for security, and a marked career. **143**

LANDON—Symbolizes the social ambitious character —proud and dignified. **725**

LAURENCE—Personifies the well trained and the successful business man. **216**

LAWRENCE—Symbolizes the courteous and progressive person. **226**

LAZARUS—Is truly the symbol of the ambitious character—but on the other hand, very generous in other matters. **142**

LEO—Represents the man of letters and sociability. **112**

LEON—Personifies the lion-hearted warrior who goes through life fearlessly. **324**

LENNIE—Is truly the personification of the mamma's boy—tender but spoiled with the motherly care and affections. **216**

LESLIE—Represents the social, ambitious but progressive person. **193**

LESTER—Personifies the prudent man. **213**

LEWIS—Symbolizes the lovable, energetic, and the successful person. **753**

LINDSIE—Symbolizes the noble and the true character. **213**

LINDY—Personifies the hero of modern times. **143**

LIONELL—Personifies the scholar and the celebrated philosopher. **163**

LOUIS—Is the symbol of purity, truth and good will towards his fellow-men. **102**

LEONARD—Symbolizes the intellectual and the well read person, who possesses a great deal of knowledge of international affairs. **936**

LEOPOLD—Symbolizes the lecturer whose colloquial talent is of the highest order. **437**

LEVI—Symbolizes the gallant forest ranger, who goes through life undaunted. **345**

LLEWELYN—Personifies the scholar and the gentleman. **223**

LUCIUS—Personifies the loyal and the progressive character. **213**

LOEB—Symbolizes the over ambitious person. **739**

LUTHER—Stands for the true and energetic fundamentalist. **237**

MACY—Is the object of self-reliance accompanied by good fortune. **344**

MALCOM—Personifies the gallant and charming hero. **183**

MARCELLUS—Stands for diversified amusements. **947**

MARCUS—Personifies the successful and intellectual organizer with a great deal of will power. **323**

MARTIN—Represents the spiritual adviser. **156**

MARX—Personifies the industrial and the commercial

propagandist. **117**

MATTHEW—Personifies the holy man. **316**

MAX—Persosifies the industrial man, with a keen sense of humor and good personality. **393**

McDONALD—Stands out for brilliance and eloquence. **315**

MICHAEL—Personifies the great spokesman and educator. **122**

MITCHEL—Personifies the successful broker. **735**

MILTON—Represents the careful and the industrious man. **371**

MORGAN—Personifies the clever business man with keen intellect. **214**

MORRIS—Symbolizes the ardent lover and the clever propagandist. It also represents the highly intellectual and the successful business man. **232**

MORTIMER—Personifies the writer and lecturer on international affairs. **711**

MOSES—Represents the holy man and the great leader. **281**

MUTT—Personifies the sportsman and the comical fellow. **194**

NAHUM—Personifies the man of a few words. **216**

NATHAN—Symbolizes the man of wealth and high position. **116**

NATHANIEL—Stands out for loyalty and good humor. **313**

NATTIE—Symbolizes the man among men. **193**

NICHOLAS—Personifies the good-natured and lovable man. **527**

NICODEMUS—Stands out for steadfastness of purpose and loyalty in every detail. **732**

NICOLA—Personifies the progressive business man **343**

NED—Stands for true friendship and a loving disposition. **923**

NORMAN—Personifies the ambitious and the industrious man. **432**

NELSON—Personifies the celebrated hero of all times. **213**

OBED—Stands out for glory and everlasting prosperity. **134**

OBEDIAH—Personifies the truthful man. **316**

ODEN—Personifies the peaceful man. **439**

OLIVER—Personifies the man of action and quick thinking. **377**

OLVIN—Represents the eloquent speaker, and the great philosopher. **219**

ORLANDO—Personifies the man with a brilliant future. **384**

OSBOURNE—Personifies the good samaritan. **126**

OSCAR—Personifies the brilliant and the successful politician. **335**

OSWALD—Personifies the man of letters and much wisdom. **636**

OTIS—Personifies the true adventurer. **511**

OWEN—Personifies tht ambitious and the prosperous business man. **332**

PAUL—Personifies the skilful and honorable man. **232**

PATRICK—Stands out for unlimited devotion. **322**

PENDRUL—Is noted for tenderness and truth. **719**

PERCIVAL—Personifies honesty, and cleverness. **253**

PINCHIE—Symbolizes the water bearer, and the clever spokesman. **211**

PERRY—Represents the industrial and the benevolent man. **284**

PETER—Personifies the true Christian. **718**

PHIL—Represents the emotional man. **223**

PHILLIE—Symbolizes the well trained entertainer and clubman. **616**

PHILLIP—Personifies the successful and the intelligent organizer. **101**

QUINCY—Is the symbol of diversified emotions. **341**

QUINTIN—Stands for courage and high endeavour. **725**

RALPH—Symbolizes the ambitious and successful man. **134**

RAYMOND—Personifies the gallant soldier of fortune. **566**

RASCUS—Is the symbol of the nobility. **234**

REGINALD—Represents the highly intellectual and well educated man with a pleasant personality. **195**

RED—Stands for courage and will power. **719**

REUBEN—Represents the man of great achievements. **235**

REUEN—Personifies the lion-hearted warrior. **101**

RICHARD—Symbolizes the great philosoher of modern times. **817**

RILEY—Personifies the talented and progressive man. **125**

ROBERT—Stands out for high endeavour and much prosperity. **618**

RODOLPHUS—Personifies the great and noble master of human frailities. **192**

RUFUS—Personifies the born ruler. **718**

RUSSELL—Stands out for sound integrity and noble action. **223**

RUTHERFORD—Symbolizes the traveler and adventurer. **277**

SAMSON—Stands out for industrial art. **324**

SAMPSON—Is noted for great strength and a great deal of endurance. **356**

SAM—Personifies the happy warrior. **136**

SAMBO—Symbolizes the ambitious and noble man. **234**

SAMUEL—Personifies the just man. **243**

SANDY—Denotes cleverness, and a keen sense of humor. **101**

SAUL—Symbolizes God's chosen. **277**

SETH—Personifies the jolly man. **316**

SHORTY—Represents the industrial and the commercial propagandist. **325**

SILAS—Stands for steadfastness of purpose and a desire to accummulate wealth. **367**

SIDNEY—Personifies the thoughtful and conservative man. **567**

SYLVESTER—Symbolizes the ardent lover and the successful business man. **101**

SIMON—Indicates the master mind of the intellectual and the wealthy class. **233**

SLIM—Is the symbol of the devoted churchman and fundamentalist. **324**

SOLOMON—Personifies the good and wise man with a tender heart, and unlimited devotion. **221**

SPOT—Stands out for courage and ability. **324**

STEWART—Is the essence of success, accompanied by the picture of good health. **011**

STANLEY—Personifies the industrial and progressive man, with a great deal of will power to reach the highest position in life. **344**

STEPHEN—Represents the energetic and the prosperous business man. **273**

SYLVESTER—Is the symbol of intelligence and ambition. **183**

THADDEUS—Personifies the man with a brilliant future. **356**

THALLES—Represents the true sportsman and clubman. **519**

THEODORE—Personifies the brilliant and the highly educated spokesman. **279**

THOMAS—Symbolizes the true and honest God fearing man, with a brilliant future. **037**

TIMOTHY—Stands for love and high endeavour. **718**

TITUS—Symbolizes the true and the noble hearted man. **215**

TOBY—Represents the man of brilliance and courage. **718**

TOM—Personifies the celebrated hero. **730**

TONY—Personifies the man of intelligence and high aspirations. **341**

URBAN—Is the main attraction of the successful and prosperous business man. **196**

URIAH—Is the symbol of the industrial and eminent man. **572**

VALENTINE—Indicates the sturdy and the highly intellectual person. **233**

VANNIE—Stands out for great success in the business world. **216**

VENIS—Personifies the thriller and the adventurer. **183**

VICTOR—Represents the great dictator and the soldier of fortune. **325**

VINCENT—Indicates great success in the professional world. **142**

WALTER—Personifies true and noble character, and a great desire to succeed in life. **108**

WALLACE—Indicates great heroism and success in the classical world. **112**

WILLARD—Symbolizes the man of international fame. **934**

WILLIAM—Personifies the intelligent and industrial man with a brilliant and a spectacular future. **324**

WILLIS—Stands out for great commercial achievements. **556**

ZACHARY—Represents the gallant warrior. **345**

ZEBEDEE—Personifies the nobility. **038**

ZACCHEUS—Is the symbol of the true sportsman and adventurer. **676**

STATES OR TERRITORY OF THE UNITED STATES

Alabama 134
Alaska 234
Arizona 711
Arkansas 213
California 184
Colorado 164
Connecticut 216
Delaware 152
District of Columbia 943
Florida 376
Georgia 153
Idaho 215
Illinois 735
Indiana 211
Indiana Territory 718
Iowa 225
Kansas 325
Kentucky 101
Louisiana 156
Maine 144
Maryland 711
Massachusetts 194
Michigan 163
Minnesota 253
Mississippi 533

Missouri 967
Mobile 161
Montana 215
Nebraska 183
Nevada 216
New Hampshire 152
New Jersey 763
New Mexico 225
New York 203
North Carolina 115
Ohio 223
Oklahoma 173
Pennsylvania 934
Rhode Island 235
St. Louis 184
South Carolina 213
South Dakota 811
Tennessee 223
Texas 976
Utah 212
Vermont 326
Virginia 523
West Virginia 411
Wisconsin 193
Wyoming 443

IMPORTANT CITIES OF THE UNITED STATES

Altantic City, N.J. 219
Allentown, Pa. 283
Altoona, Pa. 151
Atlanta, Ga. 134
Akron, Ohio 385
Augusta, Ga. 101
Aurora, Ill. 415
Baltimore, Md. 233
Bayonne, N.J. 176
Boston, Mass. 132
Buffalo, N.Y. 144
Binghamton, N.Y. 211
Birmingham, Ala. 323
Berkley, Calif. 129
Bridgeport, Conn. 119
Bròckton, Mass. 127
Bethlehem, Pa. 324
Beaumont, Tex. 719
Bay City, Mich. 518
Butte, Mont. 464
Brookline, Mass. 211
Brookline, Mass. 332
Battle Creek, Mich 145
Chicago, Ill. 365
Cleveland, Ohio 283
Cincinnati, Ohio 394
Columbus, Ohio 619
Camden, N.J. 318

Cambridge, Mass. 216
Canton, Ohio 144
Chatanooga, Tenn. 101
Cicero, Ill. 345
Covington, Ky. 276
Charlotte, N.C. 443
Cedar Rapids, Iowa 127
Charleston, W. Va. 513
Chelsea, Mass. 193
Columbus, Ga. 516
Chicopee, Mass. 311
Columbia, S.C. 176
Detroit, Mich. 314
Denver, Colo. 101
Dallas, Texas 506
Dayton, Ohio 283
Des Moines, Iowa 156
Decatur, Ill. 283
Davenport, Iowa 109
Duluth, Minn. 256
Durham, N.C. 607
Dubugue, Conn. 234
Fall River, Mass. 192
Fort Wayne, Minn. 184
Fresno, Calif. 563
East Orange, N.J. 183
El Paso, Texas 127
Elizabeth, N.J. 515

Erie, Pa. 325
East St. Louis 342
Elizabeth, N.J. 329
Elmira, N.Y. 223
Fitchburg, Mass. 718
Fort Worth, Texas 216
Flint, Mich. 345
Grand Rapids, Mich. 133
Gary, Ind. 164
Houston, Texas 181
Hamilton, Ohio 161
Harrisburg, Pa. 317
Hamtramck, 234
Highland Park, Mich. 161
Hoboken, N.J. 215
Holyoke, Mass. 364
Indianapolis, Ind. 123
Jacksonville, Fla. 619
Jersey City, N.J. 167
Johnstown, Pa. 202
Joliet, Ill. 384
Kansas City, Mo. 163
Kansas City, Kan. 101
Kenosha, Wis. 936
Knoxville, Tenn. 736
Los Angeles, Cal. 215
Lynn, Mass. 283
Lowell, Mass. 376
Little Rock, Ark. 126
Lansing, Mich. 134
Lincoln, Nebraska 617

Lakewood, N.J. 115
Lancaster, Pa. 213
Lima, Ohio 164
Lorian, Ohio 276
Manchester, N.H. 711
Milwaukee, Wis. 316
Memphis, Tenn. 345
Miami, Fla. 769
Mobile, Ala. 233
Macon, Ga. 323
Malden, Mass. 153
Mt. Vernon, N.Y. 760
McKeesport, Pa. 356
New York, N.Y. 376
Newark, N.J. 283
New Orleans, La. 215
New Haven, Conn. 314
Norfolk, Va. 342
New Bedford, Mass. 717
New Britain, Conn. 215
Oakland, Cal. 114
Omaha, Neb. 216
Oklahoma City, Okl. 333
Oak Park, Ill. 327
Pittsburgh, Pa. 314
Providence, R.I. 216
Paterson, N.J. 344
Peoria, Ill. 216
Portland, Me. 314
Passaic, N.J. 183
Pawtucket, R.I. 327

Portsmouth, Va. 676
Pasadena, Cal. 635
Pontiac, Mich. 718
Perth Amboy, N.J. 203
Pueblo, Colo. 184
Pittsfield, Mass. 657
Quincy, Mass. 313
Racine, Wis. 134
Reading, Pa. 123
Richmond, Va. 163
San Antonio, Texas 123
St. Louis, Mo. 123
Seattle, Wash. 152
Syracuse, N.Y. 739
Scranton, Pa. 515
Springfield, Mass. 112
Spokane, Wash. 117
Savannah, Ga. 283
St. Joseph, Mo. 211
Stanford, Conn. 176
Salem, Mass. 506
Saginaw, Mich 384

Springfield, Ill. 207
Shreveport, La. 505
Sioux City, Iowa 192
Stockton, Cal. 161
San Jose, Cal. 414
Trenton, N.J. 384
Tulso, Okla. 251
Tacoma, Wash. 194
Troy, N.Y. 161
Terre Haute, Ind. 234
Toledo, Ohio 173
Utica, N.Y. 113
Waco, Texas 151
Waterbury, Conn. 713
Washington, D.C. 373
Worchester, Mass. 511
Wilmington, Del. 711
Wichita, Kan. 332
Wilkes Barre, Pa. 376
Williamsport, Pa. 233
Yonkers, N.Y. 184
York, Pa. 163

YOUR HOROSCOPE

AQUARIUS—THE WATER BEARER

JANUARY 21st to FEBRUARY 19th

Persons born between these dates are ruled by the sign governing the leg of the Grand Man Aquarius— the Water Bearer. Such people are very predominant, yet they are tender and loving in every respect. They make great sacrifices in the behalfs of mankind. They generally become leaders in politics and other patriotic societies. They do well as magicians, spiritualists and ministers.

People born under this sign change their religion frequently. This is due to the fact that they wish to know the truth in order to help others spiritually as well as financially.

These people possess unlimited powers, and by so doing they acquire education easily, although they sometimes lack the ability to concentrate freely.

They are more active during the night than in the day, because their mental faculties seem to function more rapidly in the night.

They are so good natured and sympathetic, that they generally have a host of friends. Some of these friends are sincere, while others envy them for their benevolence and achievement. Therefore their friends should be well chosen.

These kind hearted people marry at an early age, which is believed to help them live such a successful life.

They generally marry with the fairer sex, yet they associate with everyone freely, regardless of race, creed or color.

Their lucky numbers are:

761,　329,　644,　580,　768,　432

Their lucky days are:

Monday, Tuesday and Thursday.

PISCES—THE FISH

FEBRUARY 20th to MARCH 21st

Persons born between February the 19th and March the 21st are governed by the neck sign of the Grand Man.

They are very polite and courteous in every respect. They are great lovers. Their love is somewhat enchanting. On account of this, they are very successful in courtship and other love affairs.

They are honest and sincere. Many of them deny themselves the comforts of life in order to help others.

These people are born artists, critics, writers, musicianers and teachers of the highest order. They also possess some magnetic powers, which make them become great thinkers and philosophers.

People born under this sign, generally live a clean life. They do not care very much for strong drinks, although they drink a little good wine now and then.

Their chief aim in life is to make others happy. This is easily seen by the life they live; always helping others in every respect.

Many of these people could become very rich if they were in the least selfish. But they are not, because they are satisfied with a comfortable life of moderate means. I must add here, that these people are very long livers.

Their lucky numbers are:

512,   269,   369,   763,   523,   725

Their lucky days are:

Monday, Tuesday and Friday.

ARIES—THE RAM

MARCH 22nd to APRIL 19th

Persons born between these dates are governed by the head sign of the Grand Man.

Persons born under this sign have a strong determination and a great amount of will power. This makes them very successful in business.

They go after things undaunted, they have no fear of any subsequent consequence. Their only desire is to succeed in life.

Their strong executive ability makes them master of all kinds of situations, regardless of how trying it happens to be. With all this, these people are very kindhearted, peaceful, generous and loving. On account of these fine qualities, they generally become benefactors.

They acquire wealth easily after they have reached their 30th birthday. Money and all kinds of wealth seem to flow to them in a natural stream of luck, as if they are endowed with some supernatural power of command.

Aries people love beautiful homes, with elaborate furnishings, the best rugs and other draperies. They have a natural desire for beautiful automobiles, motorboats, private yachts, and gay parties.

They are delighted in having a nice time among their friends and relatives.

They eat the best, drink the best, and have some of the best lovers in the world. They live an extraordinary high life.

These people generally become bankers, salesmen, storekeepers, manufacturers and real estate brokers; yet a great many of them become lawyers and doctors. They are very successful in games of chances.

Their lucky numbers are:

109,   367,   564,   467,   965,   221

Their lucky days are:

Tuesday, Friday and Saturday.

TAURUS--THE BULL

APRIL 20th to MAY 21st

People governed by this planet possess some of the very best qualities that can be found in mankind.

These people like to live a comfortable life, yet they are not greedy after money or any other material wealth. They are generally great sports, and as a result they spend money freely on their friends and other associates.

They are very unhappy for the unfortunate, and will do all that is in their power to make others happy. They generally succeed in helping their unfortunate brothers.

Tarus people generally hold good positions as nature seem to have endowed them with a natural gift of executive ability. Many of them become leaders in politics and so forth. You will find them holding other important governmental positions in the affairs of state. Many of them, are at the head of other patriotic societies. Some of them make very good social workers. They are really among the uplifting class.

Many of these people become very ferocious when they are being provoked, and in this mood they will loose their temper and cause a great deal of harm. If they would learn to govern their temper they would lead a very successful life, because they possess outstanding traits.

People ruled by this planet, generally marry at an early age. Their marriages are generally successful, although you will find a few of them among the divorce class.

Tarus people should marry with people born under the governing planet of Pisces.

Their lucky numbers are:

567,   760,   381,   642,   735,   291

Their lucky days are:

Monday, Wednesday and Saturday.

GEMINI—THE TWINS

MAY 22nd to JUNE 21st

Persons born under this planet are governed by the shoulders and hands of the Grand Man. These people are very changeable and restless; they are always planning and changing their plans. Although they change so readily, yet they suceed well in all walks of life. They become engineers, mechanics, publishers, merchants and writers. They are very active during the day. They like to sit in the summer's sun in order to enjoy the bounty of nature by beauty that bespeaks perpetual gratitude.

Many of these people marry at an early age, and settle down once for all. They make loving husbands and wives. They are much interested in home life, and as a result, they generally have very fine homes. They love luxury to their heart's content.

Their greatest ambition is wealth and power. These come to them without much effort on their part.

These people are generally very beautiful. They are tender and loving. On account of their fantastic charms, they acquire a host of friends without any effort on their part. These people are really gifted.

They are very upright in all matters. They believe in justice. Their lives are filled with sunshine, although like all people, they meet with some disappointments.

People born under this planet are radical to a certain extent. They like to have their own way in all matters. They seek knowledge of the highest order.

Their lucky numbers are:

736,   832,   805,   815,   129,   416

Their lucky days are:

Tuesday, Friday and Saturday.

CANCER—THE CRAB
JUNE 22nd to JULY 21st

Persons born under this planet are governed by the breast of the Grand Man. They are steadfast of purpose. They are interested in spiritual and social development. They believe in universal festivity and social enjoyment.

People born under this planet are fond of travels and adventures of all kinds. Their chief aim is to attain knowledge and wealth to a certain extent. They make good scholars, dentists, lawyers, physicians and so forth.

They are fond of the arts and the sciences. They love their husbands and wives and children dearly. The only fault about these people is: that they are always changing one friend for another. This seems to be a natural weakness on their part. On the other hand, they are very loving and kindhearted.

They are very jealous of their wives or husbands. Men born under this planet are very fascinating lovers. They seem to be cave men in their love affairs. They are easily attracted by the opposite sex.

These people are much happier during the day than at night. At night their thoughts wander over a vast number of things. They are always trying to get new ideas.

The greatest inventors are people born under this planet. People ruled under this sign make best marriages between the age of twenty and twenty five. They should marry with people born under their planet.

Parents should not interfere in chosing the life's mate

of their children born under this sign, for they are endowed with a sacred gift of chosing the good things of life.

These people are born lucky. Good fortune to them is nothing longing, but an ideal of existence.

Their lucky number are:

516, 367, 562, 644, 938, 739

Their lucky days are:

Tuesday, Thursday and Saturday.

LEO—THE LION

JULY 22nd to AUGUST 21st

People born under this planet are ruled by the sign governing the heart of the Grand Man. These people become great writers, thinkers, orators and architects.

They are high-minded and dignified. They dress very fascinating, and as a result, they are greatly admired and respected by all. Whether they are rich or poor they generally form the main figure of attraction.

People ruled by this sign are greatly interested in maintaining a happy and peaceful home. Their background is one of serene splendor and fantastic beauty. They are fond of dancing and other inside sports. They enjoy a little out doors sports in summer. They like to sit in the blazon sun in the spring and fall of the year.

Some of these people are very smart and cunning. They can put over the biggest proposition without any great amount of obligation on their part. They are generally successful in promoting enterprises of all description.

People born under this planet are ruled by the sun. For some reason or another, they are easily led away by the opposite sex. This seem to be one of their faults, yet it is not a serious one.

These people become angry very easily, when they are being provoked. They should receive good care and the best of training in their youth in order to offset their quick temper. They should not be teased. They should be allowed to live a quiet life.

Children born under this planet who receive good early training, become pious, good natured and sin-

Persons ruled by this sign are generally successful in dealing in stocks and bonds, buying and selling. They make fine managers and superintedents. They succeed well in all kinds of speculations. They are really the money makers, or in other words, the Gold Diggers. They can turn dross into gold.

Their lucky number are:

762,   543,   670,   573,   332,   144

Their lucky days are:

Wednesday, Thursday and Friday.

VIRGO—THE VIRGIN

AUGUST 22nd to SEPTEMBER 21st

Persons born under this planet are ruled by the sign governing the belly of the Grand Man. Such people are good natured. They have a propensity of making new acquaintances.

They make very good love matches, it seems to be their gift.

They are instrumental in uniting many a happy married couple. They are very fascinating in their dress. Men born under this planet like to live a gay and comfortable life. They love wine, women and song.

They should always seek employment in the open air. They make good engineers, salesmen, mechanics, government inspectors, farmers, aviators and so forth.

They have a strong executive ability, which make them dominate over almost everything they enter. They are always satisfied in life.

These people do not care very much about mixing with people out of their class, yet they show due reverence to all.

Women born under this planet make excellent house wives. They are very sincere to their husband. Most of them generally have beautiful children and lovely homes. They are generally satisfied in life.

These women are usually among the middle class, they get everything that they desire. This is due to the fact that they marry men of wealth and social position.

The planet under which these women are born has endowed them with such a pleasant disposition, that they can hardly help for being good.

Their lucky numbers are:

 267,   533,   201,   441,   091,   527

Their lucky days are:

Tuesday, Wednesday and Friday.

LIBRA—THE SCALES

SEPTEMBER 22nd to OCTOBER 21st

People born under this planet are governed by the loins of the Grand Man. These people are very ambitious. They also possess idomitable courage and self perseverance. When they once set their minds on accomplishing a task, nothing can stop them from succeeding.

They are very successful, as brokers, bankers, engineers and teachers. These people really belong to the middle class.

They are very unstable in love affairs. This is due to the fact that they are so fickle-minded. They are attracted by the opposite sex, and may be led away by them easily. They generally spend money freely, as they believe in having a good time among their friends.

Sometimes they possess a high sense of humor, at other times they are quick tempered; when they are being provoked, they will do much damage, for which they will be sorry afterwards. Such people should be allowed to live a quiet life.

They do not mingle into the affairs of others. For this reason, they do not wish any one to meddle into their business. They are quite able to manage and conduct all their affairs successfully.

People born under this sign like to have their own way in all matters, right or wrong, but most of the time they are right.

These people should marry between the age of twenty-five and thirty-five. If they do not marry within this limit, they stand a poor chance of being married.

They should marry with people who are governed by the ruling planet of Aries and Leo. Their marriages are generally successful.

Their lucky numbers are:

   632,   527,   619,   437,   333,   211

Their lucky days are:

Monday, Tuesday and Friday.

SCORPIO—THE SCORPION

OCTOBER 22nd to NOVEMBER 21st

Persons born under this planet are governed by the bladder and sex functions of the Grand Man.

They become great magicians, spiritualists and occult students. These people generally lead a successful life, as they are somewhat gifted.

They peer into the future, and can almost tell how a situation will materialize. Besides being of the spiritualists type, they are very successful in business of all description. The larger the business the better they succeed. They believe in doing business on a large scale. You will find many of them as Presidents and secretaries of large corporations. These people are really among the wealthy class.

People born under this planet should marry with people born under the ruling sign of Virgo—The Virgin. Men ruled under this planet love their wives very much, but on the other hand they are passionately jealous.

They do not doubt their wives, yet they have a jealous disposition which seems to be part of their nature. Apart from being jealous, they are tender and loving.

They have a pleasant personality and strong integrity. They have a natural love for their fellowmen. Their desire is to make every one as happy as possible.

There is one special comment that I must make about these people, and that is: they are generally beautiful and charming. Women born under this planet are fascinating lovers. Their beauty seem to have a tendency to make their love enchanting.

Their kisses and their caresses leave one in a sort of bewitching love stupor.

Their kisses are divine. They make successful actresses.

People ruled under this sign, adore beautiful things. They like to have swell parties, wear nice clothes and have beautiful homes. They eat and drink the very best.

They associate with the very best people, for they are upright and dignified. Social prestige is thrown upon them.

Their lucky numbers are:

769,   311,   211,   534,   691,   933

Their lucky days are:

Tuesday, Thursday and Saturday.

SAGITARIUS—THE ARCHER

NOVEMBER 22nd to DECEMBER 21st

Persons born under this sign are governed by the thighs of the Grand Man.

They are celebrated dreamers. Their dreams generally materialize within a few days. Such people should be very successful, as they have a gift of peering into the future, and even into the great beyond.

People born under this sign possess a high sense of humor. They are ambitious, courageous, and industrious. They pursue a certain course in business, and they do not stop until they reach their goal.

Their plans are generally successful, on account of the fact, that they are well laid out. They follow their own minds, for they seldom make mistakes. They can even guide others through life succesfully.

People ruled under this planet should become financiers, merchants, manufacturers, salesmen, managers, beauty culturists, and tradesmen. They should indulge in active work, or work that requires a great deal of thinking and planning. Big money to them is nothing longing, but an ideal of existence.

Children born under this planet should be allowed to chose their own life's work, for they have the gift to succeed in almost any line of business. Nothing can stand in their way of success, when they once set their minds on accomplishing a task; for they are born masters and mistresses. They are sometimes downhearted, at other times are brave, and full of life.

Persons born under this planet should marry between the age of twenty and twenty-five. They should marry with people born under the ruling planet of Leo. These marriages are generally succesful, and as a result, joy and felicity are ever present.

Their lucky numbers are:

332,   708,   478,   932,   563,   973

Their lucky days are:

Wednesday, Thursday and Saturday.

CAPRICORN—THE GOAT

DECEMBER 22nd to JANUARY 20th

Persons born under this sign are ruled by the knees of the Grand Man. Such persons become Poets, philosophers, physicians, orators and conversationalists.

They possess fine qualities. They are strictly fundamentalists. They are greatly interested in the works of nature, for they adore beauty in all forms of life.

These people are generally good natured, sympathetic and loving. They are reliable in their dealings. They despise people who are slack or fraudulent. They do not like to be in debt; they do not borrow, neither do they lend. They prefer to give; for it is a blessing to give, rather than to receive.

Persons born under this planet, generally place too much confidence in others. For this reason, they are liable to retard their progress to a certain extent. But on account of their determination, and sound integrity, they often reach the great heights and attain success.

Persons born under this sign are respected, by people of all race, creed and color. They are really the uplifting class. Their chief aim is virtue, love, and righteousness.

They are slow to anger. They sometimes forgive, but they do not forget. They are governed by Saturn.

Their lucky numbers are:

632, 563, 761, 342, 412, 112

Their lucky days are:

Tuesday, Wednesday and Friday.

Write to
G. PARRIS

P.O. Box 435
West Hempstead, N.Y. 11552

THE RELATIVE POSITION OF NUMBERS

The following sets of combinations generally follow
each other. They should be noted always.

071 is generally followed by 807 or 807 is followed
by 071. This system works both ways (vice versa).

883	by	428	390	by	960
648	"	679	542	"	428
965	"	937	172	"	167
245	"	286	368	"	789
510	"	389	998	"	935
706	"	526	505	"	962
905	"	220	254	"	252
182	"	822	439	"	982
405	"	480	464	"	186
614	"	597	573	"	937
905	"	220	172	"	312
182	"	822	660	"	760
585	"	185	300	"	350
912	"	118	498	"	769
696	"	696	338	"	772
609	"	309	497	"	287
805	"	490	364	"	409
403	"	312	883	"	807
741	"	214	393	"	889
946	"	276	352	"	926
910	"	399	340	"	406
997	"	478	276	"	666
963	"	960	212	"	869

680	by	688	063	by	367
733	"	327	642	"	285
958	"	586	496	"	500
464	"	424	357	"	532
975	"	573	582	"	908
099	"	000	266	"	416
702	"	770	534	"	485
243	"	614	298	"	408
104	"	494	403	"	312
946	"	540	552	"	712
908	"	402	698	"	498
073	"	680	007	"	099
678	"	391	293	"	029
154	"	455	129	"	393
926	"	662	835	"	501
671	"	677	546	"	717
245	"	851	083	"	904
947	"	644	390	"	196
211	"	619	298	"	749
203	"	841	900	"	209
637	"	688	862	"	703
835	"	591	544	"	234
313	"	387	889	"	013
325	"	724	123	"	855
862	"	226	405	"	091
965	"	759	506	"	690
074	"	620	367	"	569
531	"	217	776	"	252
860	"	300	679	"	163
867	"	462	427	"	842
425	"	522			

195	by	118	371	by	736
449	"	893	810	"	569
586	"	890	402	"	672
611	"	177	466	"	142
115	"	147	872	"	678
676	"	393	414	"	815
877	"	764	946	"	957
440	"	458	917	"	760
630	"	838	268	"	856
578	"	775	541	"	954
600	"	180	951	"	196
753	"	325	892	"	524
970	"	236	132	"	825
371	"	272	149	"	405
500	"	949	067	"	397
910	"	117	253	"	425
434	"	426	529	"	725
582	"	892	381	"	889
929	"	993	286	"	389
621	"	370	759	"	936
262	"	615	048	"	248
650	"	256	168	"	138
368	"	400	597	"	697
113	"	112	395	"	651
917	"	760	825	"	207
541	"	459	137	"	679
500	"	580	251	"	563
645	"	316	997	"	205
452	"	925	326	"	436
300	"	250	629	"	996

YOUR LUCKY BIRTHDAY NUMBER

JANUARY	FEBRUARY	MARCH
Jan. 1 _____ 234	Feb. 1 _____ 675	Mar. 1 _____ 616
" 2 _____ 211	" 2 _____ 384	" 2 _____ 316
" 3 _____ 623	" 3 _____ 462	" 3 _____ 715
" 4 _____ 032	" 4 _____ 781	" 4 _____ 892
" 5 _____ 532	" 5 _____ 998	" 5 _____ 777
" 6 _____ 692	" 6 _____ 771	" 6 _____ 961
" 7 _____ 416	" 7 _____ 611	" 7 _. _____ 890
" 8 _____ 590	" 8 _____ 326	" 8 _____ 010
" 9 _____ 534	" 9 _____ 332	" 9 _____ 351
" 10 _____ 490	" 10 _____ 517	" 10 _____ 725
" 11 _____ 643	" 11 _____ 896	" 11 _____ 865
" 12 _____ 213	" 12 _____ 754	" 12 _____ 256
" 13 _____ 236	" 13 _____ 110	" 13 _____ 371
" 14 _____ 312	" 14 _____ 012	" 14 _____ 879
" 15 _____ 423	" 15 _____ 636	" 15 _____ 478
" 16 _____ 804	" 16 _____ 771	" 16 _____ 816
" 17 _____ 619	" 17 _____ 118	" 17 _____ 919
" 18 _____ 531	" 18 _____ 221	" 18 _____ 345
" 19 _____ 760	" 19 _____ 354	" 19 _____ 811
" 20 _____ 408	" 20 _____ 791	" 20 _____ 119
" 21 _____ 112	" 21 _____ 865	" 21 _____ 527
" 22 _____ 245	" 22 _____ 113	" 22 _____ 165
" 23 _____ 763	" 23 _____ 201	" 23 _____ 085
" 24 _____ 572	" 24 _____ 661	" 24 _____ 416
" 25 _____ 319	" 25 _____ 954	" 25 _____ 515
" 26 _____ 915	" 26 _____ 627	" 26 _____ 718
" 27 _____ 622	" 27 _____ 531	" 27 _____ 921
" 28 _____ 317	" 28 _____ 416	" 28 _____ 356
" 29 _____ 218	" 29 _____ 515	" 29 _____ 234
" 30 _____ 219		" 30 _____ 865
" 31 _____ 936		" 31 _____ 999

Your Lucky Birthday Number

APRIL		MAY		JUNE	
Apr. 1	928	May 1	017	June 1	676
" 2	723	" 2	711	" 2	573
" 3	136	" 3	835	" 3	891
" 4	542	" 4	414	" 4	241
" 5	241	" 5	165	" 5	211
" 6	165	" 6	165	" 6	137
" 7	137	" 7	767	" 7	735
" 8	824	" 8	893	" 8	532
" 9	145	" 9	011	" 9	122
" 10	794	" 10	210	" 10	129
" 11	161	" 11	001	" 11	315
" 12	111	" 12	534	" 12	516
" 13	601	" 13	675	" 13	917
" 14	302	" 14	756	" 14	341
" 15	012	" 15	890	" 15	867
" 16	234	" 16	215	" 16	793
" 17	421	" 17	219	" 17	348
" 18	918	" 18	932	" 18	119
" 19	715	" 19	651	" 19	201
" 20	517	" 20	146	" 20	437
" 21	615	" 21	891	" 21	789
" 22	731	" 22	311	" 22	967
" 23	330	" 23	217	" 23	991
" 24	115	" 24	313	" 24	321
" 25	661	" 25	411	" 25	654
" 26	892	" 26	516	" 26	321
" 27	291	" 27	757	" 27	650
" 28	173	" 28	893	" 28	372
" 29	654	" 29	379	" 29	231
" 30	569	" 30	784	" 30	517
		" 31	819		

Your Lucky Birthday Number

JULY		AUGUST		SEPTEMBER	
July 1	199	Aug. 1	321	Sept. 1	114
" 2	653	" 2	567	" 2	743
" 3	541	" 3	354	" 3	872
" 4	721	" 4	721	" 4	930
" 5	997	" 5	997	" 5	561
" 6	238	" 6	456	" 6	716
" 7	654	" 7	409	" 7	819
" 8	143	" 8	929	" 8	215
" 9	519	" 9	673	" 9	723
" 10	562	" 10	832	" 10	601
" 11	734	" 11	138	" 11	132
" 12	869	" 12	925	" 12	259
" 13	723	" 13	561	" 13	934
" 14	167	" 14	893	" 14	853
" 15	392	" 15	819	" 15	459
" 16	740	" 16	980	" 16	317
" 17	013	" 17	756	" 17	816
" 18	415	" 18	938	" 18	215
" 19	672	" 19	291	" 19	731
" 20	374	" 20	025	" 20	934
" 21	683	" 21	732	" 21	990
" 22	493	" 22	516	" 22	112
" 23	987	" 23	617	" 23	341
" 24	392	" 24	432	" 24	412
" 25	235	" 25	293	" 25	819
" 26	345	" 26	561	" 26	239
" 27	989	" 27	721	" 27	305
" 28	751	" 28	367	" 28	607
" 29	378	" 29	532	" 29	902
" 30	645	" 30	659	" 30	104
" 31	819	" 31	919		

Your Lucky Birthday Number

OCTOBER		NOVEMBER		DECEMBER	
Oct. 1	215	Nov. 1	301	Dec. 1	185
" 2	532	" 2	133	" 2	753
" 3	432	" 3	532	" 3	831
" 4	615	" 4	961	" 4	467
" 5	731	" 5	642	" 5	654
" 6	897	" 6	235	" 6	729
" 7	734	" 7	671	" 7	816
" 8	654	" 8	432	" 8	713
" 9	543	" 9	187	" 9	642
" 10	043	" 10	987	" 10	515
" 11	321	" 11	893	" 11	312
" 12	100	" 12	315	" 12	407
" 13	908	" 13	542	" 13	759
" 14	902	" 14	869	" 14	865
" 15	531	" 15	931	" 15	212
" 16	689	" 16	837	" 16	131
" 17	496	" 17	739	" 17	754
" 18	532	" 18	921	" 18	865
" 19	788	" 19	816	" 19	490
" 20	891	" 20	523	" 20	917
" 21	375	" 21	324	" 21	819
" 22	165	" 22	816	" 22	906
" 23	761	" 23	725	" 23	110
" 24	929	" 24	220	" 24	219
" 25	333	" 25	561	" 25	256
" 26	560	" 26	715	" 26	061
" 27	731	" 27	314	" 27	934
" 28	896	" 28	543	" 28	507
" 29	759	" 29	906	" 29	965
" 30	832	" 30	533	" 30	571
" 31	327			" 31	653

THINGS THAT YOU SEE, HEAR OR HAPPENS

(Notions)

To see a fight **543**
When you are surprised **367**
To see a riot **293**
To see a black cat **414**
To see a white cat **361**
An automobile collision **537**
When you are disturbed **367**
To see a train wreck **456**
To hear of a catastrophe **511**
A funeral procession **361**
To witness a wedding **480**
When your left eye jumps **376**
When your right eye jumps **659**
When your hands itch. **980**
To see a large crowd **838**
When you get excited **392**
When your sweetheart quits **365**
When you are in love **736**
Sudden joy **342**
Sudden grief **144**

CARDS

Ace of hearts 739
Deuce of hearts 260
Trey of hearts 327
Four of hearts 287
Five of hearts 038
Six of hearts 284
Seven of hearts 965
Eight of hearts 433
Nine of hearts 827
Ten of hearts 323
Jack of hearts 395
Queen of hearts 117
King of hearts 249

Ace of clubs 101
Deuce of clubs 201
Trey of clubs 327
Four of clubs 456
Five of clubs 618
Six of clubs 732
Seven of clubs 763
Eight of clubs 981
Nine of clubs 936
Ten of clubs 459
Jack of clubs 712
Queen of clubs 361
King of clubs 540

Ace of spades 711
Deuce of spades 294
Trey of spades 360
Four of spades 281
Five of spades 843
Six of spades 328
Seven of spades 348
Eight of spades 348
Nine of spades 832
Ten of spades 565
Jack of spades 452
Queen of spades 284
King of spades 828

Ace of diamonds 611
Deuce of diamonds 744
Trey of diamonds 725
Four of diamonds 381
Five of diamonds 503
Six of diamonds 329
Seven of diamonds 821
Eight of diamonds 813
Nine of diamonds 345
Ten of diamonds 927
Jack of diamonds 384
Queen of diamonds 938
King of diamonds 492

BIRTHSTONES

Month	Stone	Symbolism
January	Garnet	Constancy, Fidelity
February	Amethyst	Sincerity
March	Bloodstone	Courage, Truthfulness
April	Diamond	Innocence
May	Emerald	Happiness
June	Pearl	Health, Long Life
July	Ruby	Contentment
August	Sardonyx	Felicity
September	Sapphire	Wisdom
October	Opal	Hope
November	Topaz	Fidelity
December	Turquoise	Prosperity, Success

Birthstones for the Days of the Week

Day	Stone
Sunday	Topaz and Diamond
Monday	Pearl and Crystal
Tuesday	Ruby and Emerald
Wednesday	Amethyst and Loadstone
Thursday	Sapphire and Carnelian
Friday	Emerald and Cat's-Eye
Saturday	Turquoise and Diamond

BIRTHDAY FLOWERS

January	Snowdrop	July	Carnation
February	Violet	August	White Heather
March	Daffodil	September	Michaelmas Daisy
April	Primrose	October	Rosemary
May	White Lily	November	Chrysanthemum
June	Wild Rose	December	Ivy

WEDDING ANNIVERSARIES

First	Paper	Thirteenth	Lace
Second	Cotton	Fourteenth	Ivory
Third	Leather	Fifteenth	Crystal
Fourth	Fruits, Flowers	Twentieth	China
Fifth	Wooden	Twenty-fifth	Silver
Sixth	Sugar, Candy	Thirtieth	Pearl
Seventh	Wool, Copper	Thirty-fifth	Coral
Eighth	Bronze, Pottery	Fortieth	Ruby
Ninth	Pottery, Willow	Forty-fifth	Sapphire
Tenth	Tin	Fiftieth	Golden
Eleventh	Steel	Fifty-fifth	Emerald
Twelfth	Silk, Linen	Seventy-fifth	Diamond

Watch How They Fall

1 6 7

7 3 5

4 9 8

8 4 8

7 6 3

4 2 1

9 3 0

7 6 8

4 7 8

4 7 4

5 7 8

7 0 5

4 4 9

3 9 0

5 9 7

6 1 6

3 1 0

1 2 8

284

286

316

716

868

898

0 3 4

0 8 0

8 0 8

7 4 6

7 3 6

9 8 9

JANUARY

1 3 4

5 1 1

8 8 0

0 6 5

7 6 9

6 9 6

FEBRUARY

5 7 6

3 1 6

9 6 2

3 6 9

4 1 4

1 1 4

MARCH

6 2 0

7 5 0

7 2 1

8 5 8

9 1 7

7 8 8

APRIL

1 8 6

0 1 2

1 0 0

6 0 7

0 3 9

4 1 2

MAY

9 2 1

7 2 9

9 3 6

8 0 6

1 3 6

0 8 4

JUNE

3 2 7

9 7 3

9 1 9

6 1 6

1 2 5

3 9 5

JULY

6 9 0

6 8 6

7 4 7

7 5 4

8 0 6

9 9 8

AUGUST

3 6 7

8 3 7

9 0 0

2 0 0

1 1 2

2 1 2

SEPTEMBER

0 8 0

1 4 9

1 4 6

4 0 2

3 9 9

5 0 9

OCTOBER

4 5 3

8 5 6

8 5 9

5 6 8

4 2 5

3 6 0

NOVEMBER

600

506

886

954

416

789

DECEMBER

3 8 1

7 3 6

5 2 7

9 3 5

6 7 6

8 2 2

$6.95

Revised and Expanded

Success and Power Through Psalms
By Donna Rose

For thousands of years, men and women have found in the Psalms the perfect prayer book, possessing wisdom applicable to every human situation. Wise men and women of deep mystical insight have also l earned to decipher the magical formulas David and the other Psalmists hid behind the written words. These formulas help the seeker solve everyday problems, achieve higher states of consciousness, gain material and spiritual wealth, as well as help defend himself or herself against psychic attacks and all manner of dangers. The Revised and Expanded edition of Donna Rose's classic offers over 300 simple to perform magical rituals to help you manifest all of your desires using the magical powers of the psalms.

WWW.OCCULT1.COM   1 (516) 605-0547

$9.95

SPIRITUAL CLEANSINGS & PSYCHIC DEFENSES

By Robert Laremy

Psychic attacks are real and their effects can be devastating to the victim. Negative vibrations can be as harmful as bacteria, germs and viruses. There are time-honored methods of fighting these insidious and pernicious agents of distress. These techniques are described in this book and they can be applied by you. No special training or supernatural powers are needed to successfully employ these remedies. All of the procedures described in this book are safe and effective, follow the instructions without the slightest deviation. The cleansings provided are intended as *"over-the-counter"* prescriptions to be used by anyone being victimized by these agents of chaos.

WWW.OCCULT1.COM   1 (516) 605-0547

$8.95

THE MAGIC CANDLE

Facts and Fundamentals of Candle Burning

By Charmaine Dey

This book contains the fundamentals of ritual candle burning and gives a complete description of:

Types of candles, Color Symbolism
Dressing and Lighting, Planning & Timing
Oils, Incenses, Seals & Parchments

The main object of this book is to help you understand what you are doing, and to create and develop your own techniques and rituals which will surely bring you the results you desire.

WWW.OCCULT1.COM   1 (516) 605-0547